PRIMARY MATHEMATICS

WORKBOOK 5B

Common Core Edition

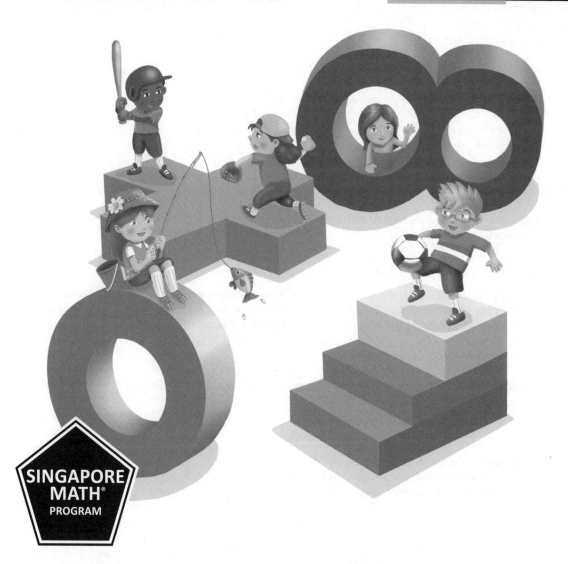

SINGAPORE MATH® PROGRAM

 **Marshall Cavendish** Education

US Distributor

 Singapore Math Inc.®

Original edition published under the title Primary Mathematics Workbook 5B
© 1981 Curriculum Planning & Development Division, Ministry of Education, Singapore
Published by Times Media Private Limited

This edition © 2014 Marshall Cavendish Education Pte Ltd
(Formerly known as Marshall Cavendish International (Singapore) Private Limited)

Published by Marshall Cavendish Education
Times Centre, 1 New Industrial Road, Singapore 536196
Customer Service Hotline: (65) 6213 9444
US Office Tel: (1-914) 332 8888 | Fax: (1-914) 332 8882
E-mail: tmesales@mceducation.com
Website: www.mceducation.com

Distributed by
Singapore Math Inc.®
19535 SW 129th Avenue
Tualatin, OR 97062, USA
Tel: (503) 557 8100
Website: www.singaporemath.com

First published 2014

Primary Mathematics (Common Core Edition) Workbook 5B
ISBN 978-981-01-9850-3

Printed in Singapore

Primary Mathematics (Common Core Edition) is adapted from Primary Mathematics Workbook 5B (3rd Edition),
originally developed by the Ministry of Education, Singapore. This edition contains new content developed by Marshall
Cavendish Education Pte Ltd, which is not attributable to the Ministry of Education, Singapore.

We would like to acknowledge the contributions by:

The Project Team from the Ministry of Education, Singapore that developed the original Singapore edition
Project Director: Dr Kho Tek Hong
Team Members: Hector Chee Kum Hoong, Liang Hin Hoon, Lim Eng Tann, Ng Siew Lee, Rosalind Lim Hui Cheng,
Ng Hwee Wan

Primary Mathematics (Common Core Edition)
Richard Askey, Emeritus Professor of Mathematics from University of Wisconsin, Madison
Jennifer Kempe, Curriculum Advisor from Singapore Math Inc.®

CONTENTS

7   Decimals

Exercise	1		5
Exercise	2		7
Exercise	3		8
Exercise	4		9
Exercise	5		10
Exercise	6		12
Exercise	7		14
Exercise	8		15
Exercise	9		17
Exercise	10		18
Exercise	11		20
Exercise	12		21
REVIEW	**7**		**23**

8   More Calculations

Exercise	1		29
Exercise	2		30
Exercise	3		32
Exercise	4		34
Exercise	5		36
Exercise	6		37
Exercise	7		39
Exercise	8		40
Exercise	9		41
REVIEW	**8**		**43**

9   Volume

Exercise	1		46
Exercise	2		49
Exercise	3		50
Exercise	4		51
Exercise	5		54
Exercise	6		55
Exercise	7		59
REVIEW	**9**		**61**

10 Average, Plots, and Graphs

Exercise	1	66
Exercise	2	70
Exercise	3	72
Exercise	4	73
Exercise	5	75
Exercise	6	77
Exercise	7	79
Exercise	8	84
REVIEW	**10**	**90**

11 Angles, Triangles, and Quadrilaterals

Exercise	1	96
Exercise	2	100
Exercise	3	102
Exercise	4	105
Exercise	5	107
Exercise	6	108
Exercise	7	109
Exercise	8	110
Exercise	9	112
Exercise	10	114
Exercise	11	115
Exercise	12	117
REVIEW	**11**	**120**

12 Percentage

Exercise	1	126
Exercise	2	128
Exercise	3	131
Exercise	4	133
Exercise	5	135
Exercise	6	137
Exercise	7	139
Exercise	8	141
REVIEW	**12**	**144**

13 Rate

Exercise	1	147
Exercise	2	149
Exercise	3	151
Exercise	4	153
REVIEW	**13**	**155**

EXERCISE 1

1. What is the value of the digit 6 in each of the following?

   (a) 1.658 ⬚

   (b) 6.185 ⬚

   (c) 3.069 ⬚

   (d) 5.746 ⬚

2. Fill in the missing numbers.

   (a) 5.04 = ⬚ ones ⬚ tenths ⬚ hundredths

   (b) 6.238 = ⬚ ones ⬚ tenths ⬚ hundredths ⬚ thousandths

3. Fill in the missing numbers.

   (a) In 3.864, the digit ⬚ is in the thousandths place.

   (b) In 49.73, the digit ⬚ is in the tenths place.

   (c) In 12.58, the value of the digit 8 is ⬚.

   (d) In 3.704, the value of the digit 4 is ⬚.

4. Write each of the following as a decimal.

   (a) 7 ones 6 tenths 2 hundredths 3 thousandths ⬚

   (b) 4 ones 6 tenths 5 thousandths ⬚

   (c) 3 hundreds 8 tens 5 thousandths ⬚

   (d) 8 ones 2 thousandths ⬚

5. (a) What number is 0.1 less than 5.609?

   (b) What number is 0.01 more than 2.809?

   (c) What number is 0.01 less than 13.520?

6. Solve each of the following.
   Write each answer as a decimal.

   (a) $0.2 + 0.04 + 0.008 =$ ☐

   (b) $0.7 + 0.09 + 0.002 =$ ☐

   (c) $3 + 0.7 + 0.08 =$ ☐

   (d) $1 + \frac{7}{10} + \frac{3}{1,000} =$ ☐

   (e) $\frac{8}{100} + \frac{5}{1,000} =$ ☐

   (f) $5 + \frac{6}{10} + \frac{9}{1,000} =$ ☐

7. Find the value of each of the following.

   (a) There are ☐ hundredths in 4.017.

   (b) 62.14 is ☐ hundredths more than 62.

   (c) 245.94 is ☐ hundredths more than 240.

8. Write each of the following as a decimal.

   (a) $2 + \frac{4}{1,000} =$ ☐

   (b) $9 \times 10^3 + 4 \times 10^2 + 2 \times \frac{1}{10^2} =$ ☐

   (c) $74 \times 10 + 42 \times \frac{1}{10^2} =$ ☐

   (d) $5 \times \frac{1}{10^2} + 1 \times \frac{1}{10^3} =$ ☐

   (e) $5 \times 10^2 + 6 + 2 \times \frac{1}{10} + 1 \times \frac{1}{10^3} =$ ☐

EXERCISE 2

1. What number does each letter represent?

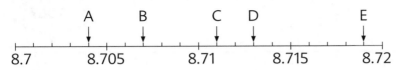

A = [   ]   B = [   ]   C = [   ]

D = [   ]   E = [   ]

2. Write >, <, or = in each ◯.

   (a) 5.89 ◯ 5.98   (b) 0.003 ◯ 0.3

   (c) 4.0 ◯ 4   (d) 3.087 ◯ 3.1

   (e) 0.7 ◯ 0.699   (f) 1.45 ◯ 1.145

3. Arrange the numbers in increasing order.

   (a) 0.008   0.09   0.08   0.009

   [   ]

   (b) 3.25   3.205   3.025   3.502

   [   ]

4. Express each decimal as a fraction in its simplest form.

(a) 0.08 =	(b) 0.14 =	(c) 0.145 =
(d) 0.408 =	(e) 4.506 =	(f) 2.6 =

EXERCISE 3

1. Fill in the missing numbers.

   (a)

   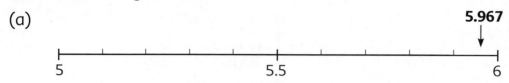

   5.967 is [ ] when rounded to the nearest whole number.

   (b) **21.504**

   21.504 is [ ] when rounded to one decimal place.

   (c) **17.006**

   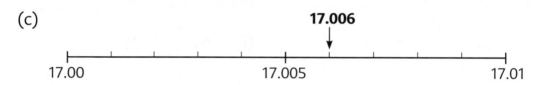

   17.006 is [ ] when rounded to two decimal places.

2. (a) Round each of the following to two decimal places.

0.079	2.307	4.084	3.255	1.802
0.008	3.023	4.035	3.661	1.206

   (b) Shade the spaces that contain the answers.
   What animal do you see?

   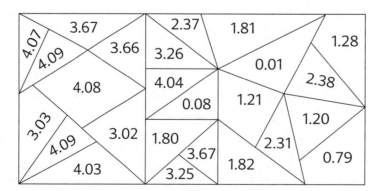

EXERCISE 4

1. Fill in the missing numbers.

   (a) $0.24 + 0.006 =$ ☐

   (b) $0.7 + 0.02 =$ ☐

   (c) $3.7 + 0.08 =$ ☐

   (d) $10.05 + 0.004 =$ ☐

   (e) $5.82 - 0.02 =$ ☐

   (f) $8.94 - 0.9 =$ ☐

   (g) $14.869 - 0.005 =$ ☐

   (h) $2.004 - 0.004 =$ ☐

2. Estimate. Then find the sum or difference.

(a) $2.398 + 46.2 \approx$	(b) $0.049 + 6.32 \approx$	(c) $5.98 + 34.086 \approx$
(d) $5.893 - 0.48 \approx$	(e) $45.9 - 3.06 \approx$	(f) $10.055 - 4.8 \approx$

EXERCISE 5

1. Multiply.

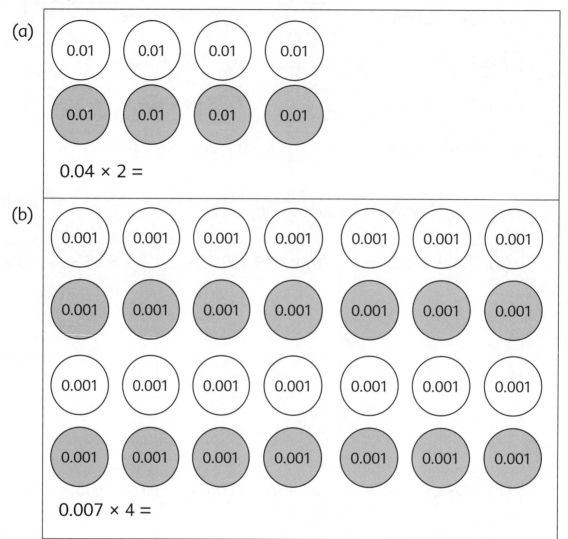

(a)

0.01 0.01 0.01 0.01

0.01 0.01 0.01 0.01

0.04 × 2 =

(b)

0.001 0.001 0.001 0.001 0.001 0.001 0.001

0.001 0.001 0.001 0.001 0.001 0.001 0.001

0.001 0.001 0.001 0.001 0.001 0.001 0.001

0.001 0.001 0.001 0.001 0.001 0.001 0.001

0.007 × 4 =

2. Multiply.

(a) 1.83 × 2 =	(b) 3.12 × 6 =
1.83 × 2	
(c) 5.21 x 3 =	(d) 6.05 x 4 =

3. Estimate. Then find the value of each of the following.

(a) 0.95 × 6 ≈	(b) 3.82 × 5 ≈	(c) 8.03 × 7 ≈
(d) 0.023 × 8 ≈	(e) 4.507 × 3 ≈	(f) 41.15 × 2 ≈
(g) 38.9 × 3 ≈	(h) 3.621 × 5 ≈	(i) 0.62 × 4 ≈
(j) 25.9 × 7 ≈	(k) 0.347 × 8 ≈	(l) 87.1 × 9 ≈

EXERCISE 6

1. Divide.

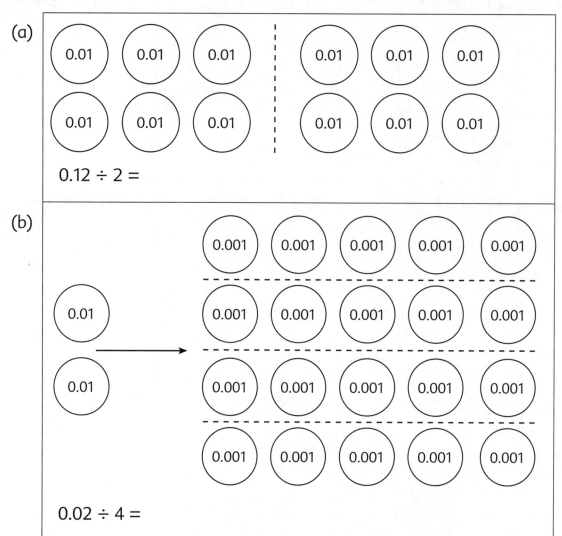

(a)

0.01 0.01 0.01   0.01 0.01 0.01

0.01 0.01 0.01   0.01 0.01 0.01

$0.12 \div 2 =$

(b)

0.01

0.01

0.001 0.001 0.001 0.001 0.001

0.001 0.001 0.001 0.001 0.001

0.001 0.001 0.001 0.001 0.001

0.001 0.001 0.001 0.001 0.001

$0.02 \div 4 =$

2. Divide.

(a) $3 \div 5 =$	(b) $0.3 \div 5 =$
(c) $1.03 \div 5 =$	(d) $6 \div 8 =$

3. Estimate. Then find the value of each of the following.

(a) $38.4 \div 3 \approx$	(b) $3.1 \div 5 \approx$	(c) $62 \div 4 \approx$
(d) $25.9 \div 7 \approx$	(e) $30 \div 8 \approx$	(f) $80.1 \div 9 \approx$
(g) $3.325 \div 5 \approx$	(h) $8.056 \div 4 \approx$	(i) $41.15 \div 2 \approx$
(j) $0.75 \div 6 \approx$	(k) $4.216 \div 8 \approx$	(l) $6.09 \div 7 \approx$

EXERCISE 7

1. Find the value of each of the following correct to one decimal place.

(a) $70 \div 9 \approx$	(b) $18.01 \div 4 \approx$
$9\overline{)70}$	

2. Find the value of each of the following correct to two decimal places.

(a) $21.68 \div 5 \approx$	(b) $41.53 \div 6 \approx$
(c) $0.53 \div 7 \approx$	(d) $24.05 \div 8 \approx$

EXERCISE 8

1. Express each fraction as a decimal correct to one decimal place.

(a) $\frac{8}{9} \approx$ $9\overline{)8}$	(b) $4\frac{1}{6} \approx$
(c) $\frac{2}{3} \approx$	(d) $5\frac{3}{7} \approx$
(e) $4\frac{5}{8} \approx$	(f) $16\frac{5}{6} \approx$

2. Express each fraction as a decimal correct to two decimal places.

(a) $\frac{2}{3} \approx$	(b) $\frac{3}{7} \approx$
(c) $5\frac{5}{8} \approx$	(d) $9\frac{1}{7} \approx$
(e) $10\frac{7}{9} \approx$	(f) $14\frac{7}{8} \approx$

3. Arrange the numbers in increasing order.

(a) $\frac{1}{3}$ 0.34 $\frac{2}{7}$ 0.3

(b) 0.657 $\frac{2}{3}$ $\frac{5}{9}$ 0.567

EXERCISE 9

1. Multiply.

(a) 0.03 × 10 = [   ]   (b) 0.009 × 10 = [   ]

(c) 0.067 × 10 = [   ]   (d) 0.84 × 10 = [   ]

(e) 2.9 × 10 = [   ]   (f) 0.321 × 10 = [   ]

(g) 5.24 × 10 = [   ]   (h) 35.4 × 10 = [   ]

(i) 6.015 × 10 = [   ]   (j) 412.8 × 10 = [   ]

2. Multiply.

(a) 0.09 × 20 = 0.18 × 10

  =

0.09 × 2 = 0.18

(b) 3.2 × 40 =

(c) 4.63 × 60 =

(d) 22.9 × 80 =

(e) 12.4 × 90 =

EXERCISE 10

1. Complete the table.

Number	× 10	× 100	× 1,000
0.324			
1.635			
3.004			
8.19			
20.4			

2. Multiply.

(a) $6.166 \times 100 =$ [　　　]

(b) $2.009 \times 10^2 =$ [　　　]

(c) $100 \times 5.201 =$ [　　　]

(d) $10^2 \times 3.065 =$ [　　　]

(e) $0.072 \times 1,000 =$ [　　　]

(f) $8.625 \times 10^3 =$ [　　　]

(g) $10^3 \times 4.86 =$ [　　　]

(h) $1,000 \times 3.7 =$ [　　　]

3. Fill in the missing numbers.

(a) $2.68 \times$ [　　　] $= 26.8$

(b) [　　　] $\times 0.8 = 8$

(c) $1.042 \times$ [　　　] $= 104.2$

(d) [　　　] $\times 1.43 = 1,430$

(e) $32.64 \times$ [　　　] $= 326.4$

(f) [　　　] $\times 0.9 = 900$

(g) $4.125 \times$ [　　　] $= 4,125$

(h) [　　　] $\times 3.95 = 395$

(i) $6.9 \times$ [　　　] $= 690$

(j) [　　　] $\times 0.731 = 731$

4. Multiply.

(a) 0.06 × 200 = 0.12 × 100
            =

0.06 × 2 = 0.12

(b) 0.34 × 300 =

(c) 6.8 × 400 =

(d) 3.12 × 500 =

(e) 64.5 × 6,000 =

(f) 32.08 × 7,000 =

(g) 9.54 × 8,000 =

(h) 3.24 × 9,000 =

EXERCISE 11

1. Divide.

   (a) 6 ÷ 10 = ☐   (b) 0.3 ÷ 10 = ☐

   (c) 0.05 ÷ 10 = ☐   (d) 0.34 ÷ 10 = ☐

   (e) 1.2 ÷ 10 = ☐   (f) 19 ÷ 10 = ☐

   (g) 20.5 ÷ 10 = ☐   (h) 3.65 ÷ 10 = ☐

   (i) 239 ÷ 10 = ☐   (j) 0.58 ÷ 10 = ☐

2. Divide.

(a) 0.8 ÷ 20 = 0.4 ÷ 10 =	0.8 ÷ 2 = 0.4 
(b) 3.7 ÷ 50 =	
(c) 5.34 ÷ 60 =	
(d) 82.08 ÷ 90 =	
(e) 29.61 ÷ 70 =	

EXERCISE 12

1. Complete the table.

Number	÷ 10	÷ 100	÷ 1,000
203			
8			
7,050			
58			
1,458			

2. Divide.

(a) $54 \div 100 =$

(b) $20.3 \div 10^2 =$

(c) $2,820 \div 100 =$

(d) $3.4 \div 10^2 =$

(e) $4,525 \div 1,000 =$

(f) $3,400 \div 10^3 =$

(g) $73 \div 10^3 =$

(h) $2 \div 1,000 =$

3. Fill in the missing numbers.

(a) $6.7 \div \boxed{} = 0.67$

(b) $80 \div \boxed{} = 0.8$

(c) $5,040 \div \boxed{} = 5.04$

(d) $56.8 \div \boxed{} = 0.568$

(e) $29 \div \boxed{} = 0.029$

(f) $3.18 \div \boxed{} = 0.318$

(g) $153 \div \boxed{} = 1.53$

(h) $900 \div \boxed{} = 0.9$

(i) $46 \div \boxed{} = 4.6$

(j) $608 \div \boxed{} = 0.608$

4. Divide.

(a) $7.2 \div 200 = 3.6 \div 100$ $\qquad = $  $\boxed{7.2 \div 2 = 3.6}$
(b) $9 \div 300 = $
(c) $95.4 \div 900 = $
(d) $57.6 \div 800 = $
(e) $18 \div 6{,}000 = $
(f) $65 \div 5{,}000 = $
(g) $392 \div 4{,}000 = $
(h) $847 \div 7{,}000 = $

REVIEW 7

1. Write each of the following as a decimal.

    (a) $8 + \frac{3}{1,000} + \frac{6}{10}$

    (b) $\frac{2}{100} + \frac{6}{10} + 5 + \frac{9}{1,000}$

    (c) $7 \times 10^3 + 5 \times 10^2 + 1 \times 10 + 7 + 3 \times \frac{1}{10^2}$

    (d) $6 \times 10^3 + 4 \times 10 + 2 + 6 \times \frac{1}{10} + 5 \times \frac{1}{10^3}$

2. What number must be added to 0.463 to give the answer 1?

3. (a) What number is 0.01 more than 6.99?

    (b) What number is 0.01 less than 4.2?

4. Fill in the missing numbers.

    (a) $5.012 = 5 + \dfrac{\boxed{}}{100} + \dfrac{2}{1,000}$

    (b) $2.004 = 2 + \dfrac{4}{\boxed{}}$

    (c) $16.27 = 16 + \dfrac{2}{\boxed{}} + \dfrac{7}{\boxed{}}$

5. Fill in the box with a decimal.

    $39.105 = 39 + \boxed{}$

6. Look at the following numbers.

    3.016   360.1   3.601   36.01   3.061   3601

    (a) Which number is the smallest?

    (b) Which number has the digit 6 in the tenths place?

    (c) In which number does the digit 6 stand for 6 hundredths?

7. Find the value of each of the following.

   (a) In 50.163, the value of the digit 6 is equal to 6 × [   ].

   (b) 83.21 is [   ] hundredths more than 83.

   (c) 395.62 is [   ] thousandths more than 390.

8. Find the value of each of the following.

   (a) 7.12 × 10   [   ]

   (b) 5.6 ÷ 100   [   ]

   (c) 60.4 ÷ 10^2 [   ]

   (d) 0.012 × 10^3 [   ]

   (e) 0.56 ÷ 40   [   ]

   (f) 0.006 × 3,000   [   ]

9. Find the value of each of the following.

   (a) 4.56 + 36.1   [   ]

   (b) 23.5 − 0.21   [   ]

10. Express $2\frac{4}{9}$ as a decimal correct to two decimal places.   [   ]

11. Write >, <, or = in each ◯.

    (a) 4.79 ◯ 4.8   (b) 1.04 ◯ 1.004

    (c) 9.1 ◯ 9.10   (d) 8.099 ◯ 8.1

12. Arrange the numbers in increasing order.

    (a) 4.386   4.638   4.683   4.9

    (b) 10   9.932   9.392   9.923

    (c) $3\frac{1}{3}$ 3.5 $3\frac{3}{4}$ 3.05

13. Express each decimal as a fraction in its simplest form.

    (a) 0.55

    (b) 5.56

    (c) 0.095

    (d) 9.008

14. Find the value of each of the following correct to two decimal places.

(a) $40.3 + 0.438 =$	(b) $16.53 - 7.174 =$	(c) $8 \times 3.251 =$
(d) $9.03 \div 4 =$	(e) $3.45 \times 9.3 =$	(f) $34.65 \div 4.7 =$

15. What number does each letter represent?

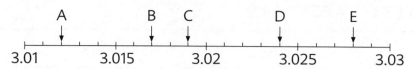

A = [____]   B = [____]   C = [____]

D = [____]   E = [____]

16. Which one of the following numbers is 4 when rounded off to the nearest whole number?

3.75,   3.07,   4.52,   4.99

[____]

17. Write **−**, **+**, **×**, or **÷** in each ◯.

(a) 82.72 ◯ 10 = 72.72

(b) 4.6 ◯ 100 = 104.6

(c) 3.64 ◯ 10 = 36.4

(d) 28.6 ◯ 100 = 0.286

(e) 5.92 ◯ 0.1 = 0.592

(f) 83.3 ◯ 0.1 = 833

18. Find the product of 34.09 and 8,000.

[____]

19. Mrs. Chen poured 5 L of syrup equally into 8 jugs. How much syrup was there in each jug? Give the answer in liters correct to two decimal places.

[____]

20.

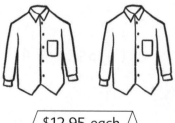

$12.95 each

$8.75 each

Jean bought 2 shirts and 3 T-shirts.
How much did she pay altogether?

[____]

21. Adam bought 8 notepads at $1.45 each and 10 towels.
    He gave the cashier $100 and received $46 change.
    Find the cost of each towel.

---

22. Ivan bought 8 oranges and 6 pears.
    The cost of each orange is $0.45.
    A pear cost twice as much as an orange.
    How much did he pay altogether?

23. Maria has 30 m of raffia. She used 3.15 m to tie a package. She cut the remaining part of raffia equally into 6 pieces to make flowerpot holders. How much raffia did she use for each flowerpot holder? Give your answer in meters correct to two decimal places.

---

24. Adam mixed 3.46 kg of hazel nuts with twice as many kilograms of almond nuts. He packed the mixture into 9 bags. How many kilograms of nuts were there in each bag? Give your answer in kilograms correct to one decimal place.

EXERCISE 1

1. Estimate the value of each of the following.

(a) $39.57 \times 48 \approx 40 \times 50$

$= $

(b) $21.68 \times 61 \approx$

(c) $42.07 \times 32 \approx$

(d) $68.35 \times 29 \approx$

(e) $52.46 \times 38 \approx$

EXERCISE 2

1. Multiply.

(a) 4.8 × 23 = 4.8 × 23 ‾‾‾‾‾‾	(b) 6.51 × 37 =
(c) 23.97 × 52 =	(d) 705.8 × 45 =
(e) 0.59 × 86 =	(f) 3.09 × 34 =
(g) 16.47 × 91 =	(h) 72.15 × 67 =

2. Multiply.

(a)   1.8
    × 12
	(b) 0.74
	    × 34
		(c) 2.53
		    × 29

(d)   46.6
    ×   67
	(e) 0.92
	    × 53
		(f) 0.58
		    × 91

(g)   1.86
    ×   25
	(h) 7.39
	    × 48
		(i) 42.08
		    × 36

Shade the spaces that contain the answers to the above.
You will find the prize Andrew won.

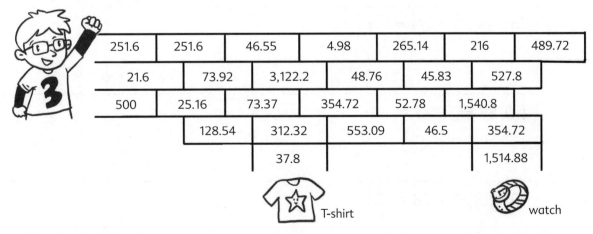

251.6	251.6	46.55	4.98	265.14	216	489.72
21.6	73.92	3,122.2	48.76	45.83	527.8	
500	25.16	73.37	354.72	52.78	1,540.8	
	128.54	312.32	553.09	46.5	354.72	
		37.8			1,514.88	

T-shirt   watch

Andrew won a _____.

EXERCISE 3

1. Estimate the value of each of the following.

(a) $5,026 \div 10 \approx 5,000 \div 10$
$$=$$

(b) $502.6 \div 10 \approx$

(c) $50.26 \div 10 \approx$

(d) $5.026 \div 10 \approx$

(e) $308.26 \div 14 \approx$

(f) $711.85 \div 17 \approx$

(g) $53.08 \div 29 \approx$

(h) $83.66 \div 13 \approx$

(i) $2.999 \div 28 \approx$

2. Find the value of each of the following correct to two decimal places.

(a) $5.4 \div 15 =$	(b) $12.05 \div 12 =$
(c) $45.28 \div 21 =$	(d) $105.22 \div 30 =$
(e) $0.83 \div 11 =$	(f) $11.58 \div 40 =$

EXERCISE 4

Multiply.

1.

(a) $0.7 \times 0.1 = \dfrac{7}{10} \times \dfrac{1}{10}$

$= \dfrac{\square}{100}$

(b) $0.02 \times 0.1 =$

(c) $0.05 \times 0.1 =$

(d) $9 \times 0.1 =$

2. Multiply.

(a) $18 \times 0.1 =$

(b) $6.9 \times 0.1 =$

(c) $57.3 \times 0.1 =$

(d) $0.11 \times 0.01 =$

(e) $42.5 \times 0.01 =$

3. Multiply.

(a) $1.78 \times 0.2 = 1.78 \times 2 \times 0.1$

$= \underline{\hspace{2cm}} \times 0.1$

$= \underline{\hspace{2cm}}$

(b) $3.54 \times 0.5 =$

(c) $8.63 \times 0.7 =$

4. Estimate. Then multiply.

(a) $3.9 \times 0.7 \approx 4 \times 0.7$ $= \underline{\hspace{2cm}}$ $3.9 \times 0.7 = \underline{\hspace{2cm}}$	(b) $4.65 \times 0.5 \approx$
(c) $55.2 \times 0.3 \approx$	(d) $0.87 \times 0.6 \approx$
(e) $1.7 \times 0.02 \approx$	(f) $2.51 \times 0.9 \approx$
(g) $78.3 \times 0.06 \approx$	(h) $0.21 \times 0.4 \approx$

EXERCISE 5

1. Estimate the value of each of the following.

(a) $19.7 \times 0.72 \approx 20 \times 0.7$ $= \underline{\hspace{2cm}}$	(b) $38.56 \times 0.45 \approx$
(c) $99.7 \times 0.99 \approx$	(d) $214.5 \times 8.72 \approx$

2. Multiply.

(a) $9.54 \times 4.2 =$	(b) $43.21 \times 1.9 =$
(c) $6.8 \times 28 =$	(d) $7.25 \times 0.12 =$
(e) $9.7 \times 0.31 =$	(f) $0.37 \times 59 =$

EXERCISE 6

1. Divide.

(a) 800 ÷ 0.1 =	(b) 90 ÷ 0.1 =
(c) 7 ÷ 0.1 =	(d) 0.6 ÷ 0.1 =
(e) 30 ÷ 0.01 =	(f) 0.2 ÷ 0.01 =
(g) 4 ÷ 0.001 =	(h) 0.08 ÷ 0.001 =
(i) 0.009 ÷ 0.001 =	(j) 0.007 ÷ 0.001 =

2. Estimate the value of each of the following.

(a) $54.89 \div 0.2 \approx 50 \div 0.2$ $= 500 \div 2$ $=$	(b) $44.44 \div 0.5 \approx$
(c) $1.187 \div 0.04 \approx$	(d) $7.39 \div 0.06 \approx$

3. Find the value of each of the following correct to at most two decimal places.

(a) $56.7 \div 0.2 =$	(b) $65.65 \div 0.06 =$
(c) $325 \div 0.004 =$	(d) $200 \div 0.007 =$

EXERCISE 7

1. Estimate the value of each of the following.

(a) $7,690 \div 11.3 \approx 7,700 \div 11$ $=$	(b) $251 \div 0.53 \approx 250 \div 0.5$ $= 2,500 \div 5$ $=$
(c) $369.2 \div 0.48 \approx$	(d) $41.82 \div 0.065 \approx$
(e) $80.96 \div 0.086 \approx$	(f) $1.01 \div 0.010 \approx$

2. Find the value of each of the following correct to at most two decimal places.

(a) $67.9 \div 1.2 =$	(b) $24.89 \div 0.13 =$
(c) $7.1 \div 0.08 =$	(d) $34 \div 0.007 =$

EXERCISE 8

1. Find the equivalent measures.

(a) 0.4 km = _____ m	(b) 1.5 km = _____ m
(c) 0.09 kg = _____ g	(d) 0.43 m = _____ cm
(e) 1.25 ft = _____ ft _____ in.	(f) 4.5 lb = _____ lb _____ oz
(g) 3.04 km = _____ km _____ m	(h) 3.8 L = _____ L _____ ml

EXERCISE 9

1. Find the equivalent measures. Express each answer as a decimal.

(a) 6 g = _____ kg	(b) 8 cm = _____ m
(c) 40 ml = _____ L	(d) 54 m = _____ km
(e) 2 kg 300 g = _____ kg	(f) 3 m 50 cm = _____ m
(g) 4 km 30 m = _____ km	(h) 2 L 600 ml = _____ L

2. Find the equivalent measures. Express each answer as a decimal.

(a) 250 cm = _____ m	(b) 1,080 g = _____ kg
(c) 3,006 m = _____ km	(d) 2,400 g = _____ kg
(e) 14 c = _____ qt	(f) 345 cm = _____ m
(g) 231 in. = _____ ft	(h) 3,245 ml = _____ L

REVIEW 8

1. Estimate the value of each of the following.

(a) 49.62 × 37 ≈	(b) 2.384 ÷ 0.06 ≈
(c) 627.8 × 58 ≈	(d) 34.65 ÷ 0.5 ≈

2. Write × or ÷ in each ◯.

   (a) 5.92 ◯ 0.1 = 0.592

   (b) 83.3 ◯ 0.1 = 833

3. Find the value of each of the following.

(a) 4.08 × 65 =	(b) 49.92 ÷ 16 =
(c) 63.2 × 4.5 =	(d) 459 ÷ 0.8 =
(e) 37.24 × 2.8 =	(f) 48.14 ÷ 8.3 =

4. Find the product of 34.9 and 8.1.

5. Find the quotient of 50.04 ÷ 0.9.

6. Divide 80 by 0.01.

7. Multiply 3.72 by 0.7.

8. Find the value of each of the following correct to two decimal places.

(a) 34.9 ÷ 62

(b) 3.45 × 9.3

(c) 34.65 ÷ 4.7

9. Find the equivalent measures.

(a) 5 km 60 m = [ ] km

(b) 34 ft 9 in. = [ ] ft

(c) 6 kg 200 g = [ ] kg

(d) 4 h 18 min = [ ] h

10. Which is the greatest in value?
    2.5 ft, 37 in., 2.25 ft, 0.5 yd

11. Fill in the missing numbers.

(a) 0.01 × [ ] = 10

(b) [ ] ÷ 0.7 = 136

12. Arrange the numbers in increasing order.

(a) 0.75 lb   11 oz $\frac{13}{16}$ lb

(b) 16 qt   1.5 gal   10 qt

(c) 39 in. $1\frac{2}{3}$ yd   3.2 ft

13. Fill in the missing numbers.

(a) 4.25 qt = ☐ c

(b) 0.8 kg = ☐ g

(c) 0.37 km = ☐ m

(d) 8.2 h = ☐ min

(e) 25 cm = ☐ m

(f) 2,400 g = ☐ kg

(g) 54 in. = ☐ ft

14. A bottle contains 1.2 L of fruit juice. Express the amount of fruit juice in milliliters.   ☐

15. The total weight of 5 bars of chocolate and a bag of sugar is 3.4 lb. If the weight of the bag of sugar is 1.1 lb, find the weight of each bar of chocolate.   ☐

16. Mrs. Meyer jogs 0.75 mi a day. If she jogs the same distance daily, how many miles does she jog in 12 days?   ☐

EXERCISE 1

1. Which of the following solids are rectangular prisms?

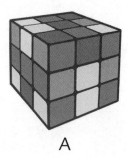

A

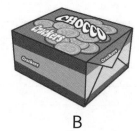

B

C

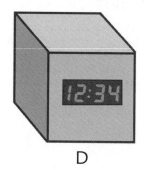

D

E

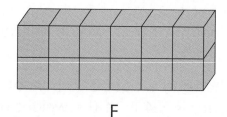

F

2. The following solids are made up of 1-cm cubes.
   Find the volume of each solid.

(a)

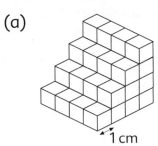

1 cm

Volume = [＿＿＿＿＿] cm³

(b)

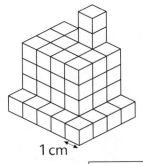

1 cm

Volume = [＿＿＿＿＿] cm³

(c)

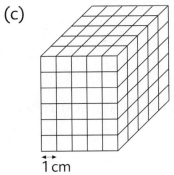

1 cm

Volume = [＿＿＿＿＿] cm³

(d)

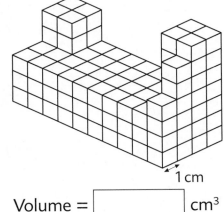

1 cm

Volume = [＿＿＿＿＿] cm³

3. The following solids are made up of 1-cm cubes. How many more cubes are needed to make each solid a rectangular prism that measures 5 cm by 4 cm by 4 cm?

(a)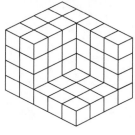

Cubes needed = ☐

(b)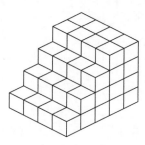

Cubes needed = ☐

(c)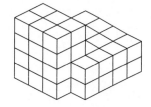

Cubes needed = ☐

(d)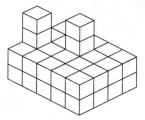

Cubes needed = ☐

4. How many 1-cm cubes are needed to fill a rectangular container that measures 3 cm by 3 cm by 4 cm?

EXERCISE 2

1. Find the volume of each rectangular prism.

(a)

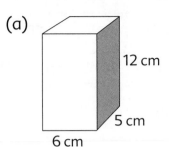

12 cm

5 cm

6 cm

(b)

17 cm

12 cm

23 cm

Volume = [   ] cm³   Volume = [   ] cm³

(c)

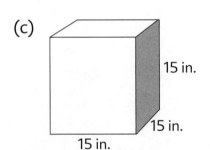

15 in.

15 in.

15 in.

(d)

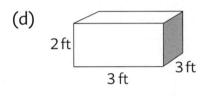

2 ft

3 ft

3 ft

Volume = [   ] in.³   Volume = [   ] ft³

2. How many 1-cm cubes are needed to fill a rectangular container that is 15 cm long, 9 cm wide, and 7 cm high?

EXERCISE 3

1. Write the volume in cubic centimeters.

   (a) 4.5 L = [ ] cm³　　(b) 0.25 L = [ ] cm³

   (c) 0.08 L = [ ] cm³　　(d) $\frac{3}{4}$ L = [ ] cm³

2. Write the volume in liters.

   (a) 5,600 cm³ = [ ] L　　(b) 450 cm³ = [ ] L

   (c) 20 cm³ = [ ] L　　(d) 12,000 cm³ = [ ] L

3. Write the volumes in liters.

(a) 12 cm　20 cm　5 cm The volume of the water is _____.	(b) 12 cm　30 cm　10 cm The volume of the water is _____.
(c) 30 cm　12 cm　10 cm The volume of the water is _____.	(d) 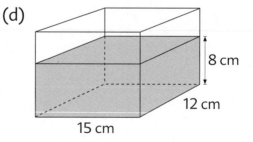 15 cm　12 cm　8 cm The volume of the water is _____.

EXERCISE 4

1. A solid is made up of 2 cubes, one on top of the other. The top cube has sides of 12 cm and the bottom cube has sides of 18 cm. What is the volume of the solid?

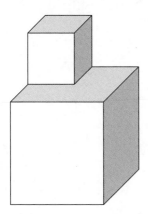

---

2. Find the volume of water needed to fill the container.

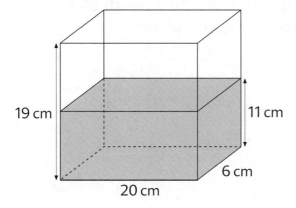

3. (a) Find the volume of the container.

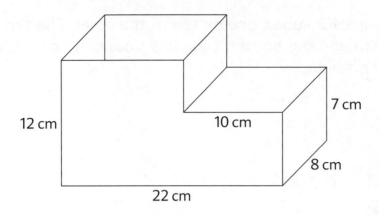

12 cm

22 cm

10 cm

7 cm

8 cm

(b) The container in (a) is filled with water to a depth of 10 cm. What is the volume of water in the container?

4. The container shown is filled with water to a depth of 9 cm. How much water does it contain?

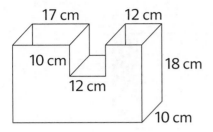

17 cm   12 cm
10 cm
12 cm
18 cm
10 cm

5. A rectangular container has a square hole through its center. It is $\frac{1}{2}$-filled with water. How much water does it contain?

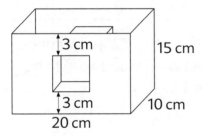

3 cm
15 cm
3 cm   10 cm
20 cm

EXERCISE 5

1. Find the volume of each rectangular prism.

    (a)

    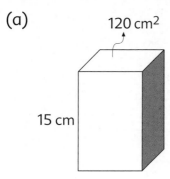

    120 cm²

    15 cm

    (b)

    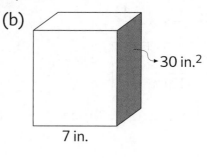

    30 in.²

    7 in.

    Volume = [＿＿＿＿] cm³   Volume = [＿＿＿＿] in.³

2. The base area of this tank is 84.5 cm².
    What is the volume of water in the tank?

    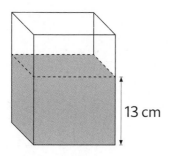

    13 cm

---

3. In order to completely cover the bottom of a box, 72 1-cm cubes
    are used. Then 8 more layers of 1-cm cubes are added to fill the
    box completely. What is the volume of the box?

EXERCISE 6

1. Find the length of one edge of the cube.

Volume = 64 cm³

2. Find the unknown edge of each of the following solids.

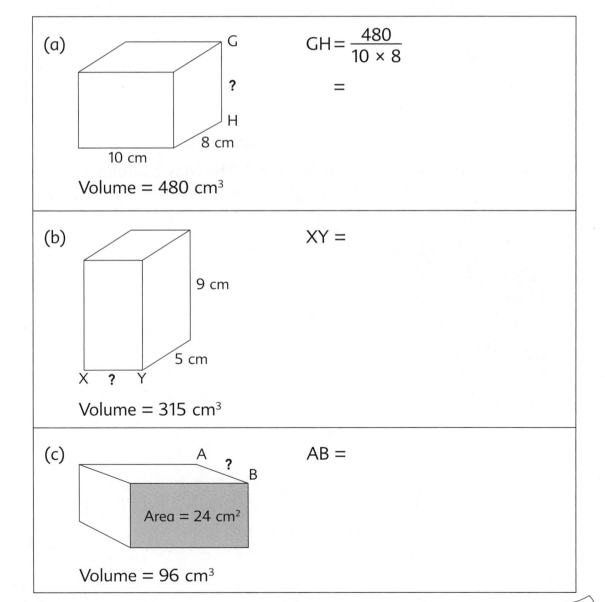

(a)

G

?

H

8 cm

10 cm

Volume = 480 cm³

$$GH = \frac{480}{10 \times 8}$$

$$=$$

(b)

9 cm

5 cm

X   ?   Y

Volume = 315 cm³

$XY =$

(c)

A   ?   B

Area = 24 cm²

Volume = 96 cm³

$AB =$

3. The base of a rectangular container measures 20 cm by 15 cm.
    The container contains 900 cm³ of water. What is the height of the
    water level in the container?

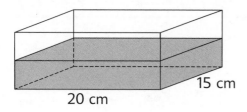

20 cm   15 cm

4. The base of a rectangular tank is 6 m². The tank contains
    15 m³ of water. What is the height of the water level in the tank?

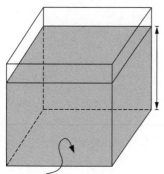

Base area = 6 m²

5. A rectangular container measuring 12 in. by 10 in. by 11 in. is completely filled with water. After 240 in.³ of water are taken out of the container, what is the height of the water level?

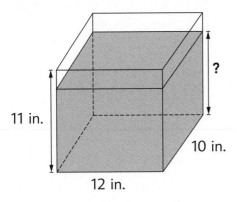

11 in.

?

10 in.

12 in.

6. A rectangular tank, 40 cm long and 25 cm wide, contains water to a depth of 15 cm. After 2 L of water are taken out of the tank, what is the height of the water level in the tank? (1 L = 1,000 cm³)

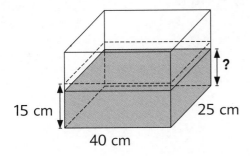

15 cm

?

25 cm

40 cm

7. A rectangular tank with a base area of 600 cm² and a height of
    33 cm is filled with water to a height of 18 cm. How many liters of
    water are needed to fill the tank completely?

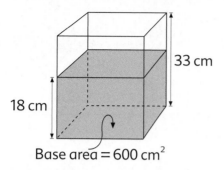

33 cm

18 cm

Base area = 600 cm²

---

8. A rectangular tank has a base 16 cm by 11 cm and a height of 36 cm.
    It is partly filled with water to a height of 12 cm. How much water

    has to be poured out so that it is only $\frac{1}{4}$ full?
    Express the answer in milliliters.

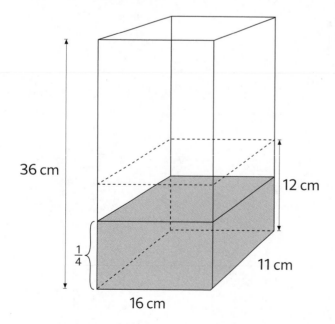

36 cm

12 cm

$\frac{1}{4}$

11 cm

16 cm

EXERCISE 7

1. A rectangular container, 20 cm long and 15 cm wide, contained some water. When an iron ball was put in, the water level rose by 3 cm. Find the volume of the iron ball.

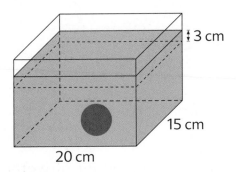

2. A rectangular container, 20 cm long and 10 cm wide, contained some water and a stone. When the stone was taken out, the water level dropped from 12 cm to 10 cm. Find the volume of the stone.

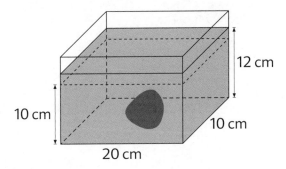

3. A rectangular tank is 20 cm long and 15 cm wide. It is filled with water to a depth of 20 cm. When a stone of volume 600 cm³ is placed in the tank, the water level rises. Find the height of the new water level.

4. Two identical containers, A and B, have the same amount of water. After placing 4 marbles into Container A and 3 metal cubes into Container B, the water levels in both containers rose to the same level. When a marble is transferred from Container A to Container B, the total volume of water, marble, and cubes in Container B is 300 cm³ more than the total volume of water and marbles in Container A. Find the volume of each cube.

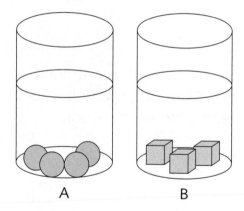

A   B

REVIEW 9

1. The following solid is made up of 2-cm cubes.
   Find its volume.

   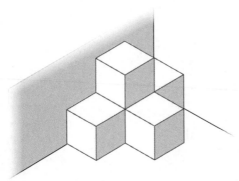

2. Find the volume of each rectangular prism.

   (a)

   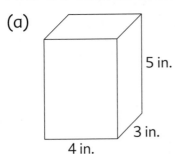

   5 in.
   3 in.
   4 in.

   (b)

   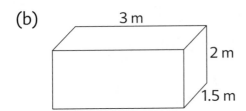

   3 m
   2 m
   1.5 m

3. The volume of a tank is 480 cm³.
   It is 12 cm long and 8 cm wide.
   Find its height.

4. A tank is 2 m long, 2 m wide, and 5 m high.
   It is $\frac{2}{5}$- filled with water.
   How much water is in the tank?

   [ ]

5. Fill in the missing numbers.

   (a) 1.07 L = [ ] cm³

   (b) 4,500 ml = [ ] cm³

   (c) 75 cm³ = [ ] L [ ] mL

   (d) 9,030 cm³ = [ ] L

6. Find the volume of the solid.

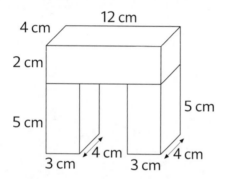

   [ ]

7. A wooden block has a rectangular hole through its center. Find the volume of the block.

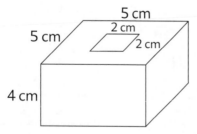

   [ ]

8. The volume of a tank is 1,080 in.³.
   If the base has an area of 72 in.²,
   what is the height?

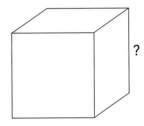

9. The volume of a cube is 216 cm³.
   Find the length of each edge.

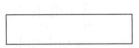

10. A rectangular tank, 11 m long and 9 m wide,
    contains 495 m³ of water when it is full.
    Find the height of the tank.

11. A tank, 40 cm by 30 cm by 20 cm, is filled with
    water to its brim. If 2.4 L of water is poured out
    from the container, what will be the height of the
    new water level?

12. A rectangular container measuring 70 cm by 30 cm by 20 cm is $\frac{1}{2}$ full. How much water is needed to fill it to the height of 15 cm? Express the answer in liters.

13. A rectangular container measuring 40 cm by 30 cm by 24 cm is $\frac{3}{4}$ full. If 15 L of water are poured into the tank, how much water would spill over? Express the answer in liters.

14. A rectangular tank measuring 12 in. by 8 in. by 15 in. is filled with water to the depth of 10 in. When 8 similar marbles were placed in the tank, the water level became 12 in. Find the volume of each marble. (Assume all the marbles are completely under water.)

---

15. A rectangular tank measuring 30 cm by 30 cm by 42 cm is $\frac{1}{3}$ full. When a metal ball was placed in the container, it became $\frac{6}{7}$ full. What was the volume of the metal ball? (Assume the metal ball is completely under water.)

EXERCISE 1

1. Find the average of each of the following.

(a) 3, 8, and 7

$3 + 8 + 7 = 18$

The sum is _____.

$18 ÷ 3 =$

The average is _____.

(b) 45 and 33

(c) 24, 38, and 19

(d) 20, 18, 36, and 98

---

2. The picture graph shows the number of kites made by 4 boys.

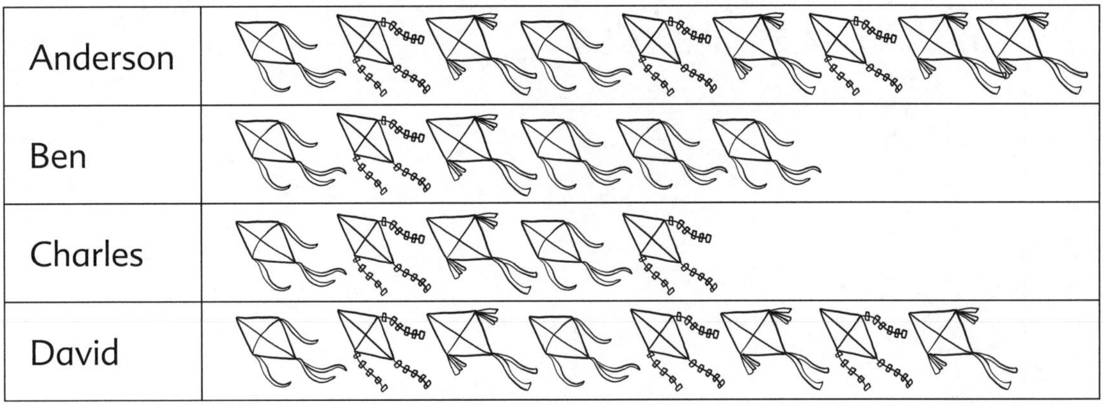

Anderson	🪁🪁🪁🪁🪁🪁🪁🪁
Ben	🪁🪁🪁🪁🪁
Charles	🪁🪁🪁🪁
David	🪁🪁🪁🪁🪁🪁🪁

Find the average number of kites each boy made.

---

3. The table shows the amount of money saved by 4 girls.

Devi	Maria	Meiling	Lily
$25	$18	$32	$29

Find their average savings.

4. Find the average of each of the following.

(a) $3.70, $4.25, and $4.50

(b) 12.5 m, 14.7 m, and 12.4 m

(c) 15.5 kg, 12 kg, 14.3 kg, and 16.6 kg

(d) 430 L and 22 L

5. The table shows the shot put results of 4 boys.
    Find the average distance.

Ian	3.8 yd
Adam	5 yd
Pablo	5.42 yd
Jim	4.5 yd

6. Find the average weight of the papayas.

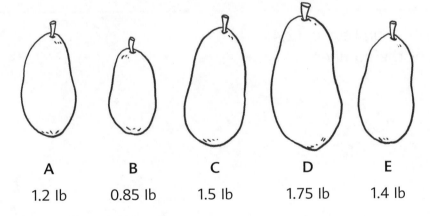

A	B	C	D	E
1.2 lb	0.85 lb	1.5 lb	1.75 lb	1.4 lb

EXERCISE 2

1. From Monday to Wednesday, Alex sold 258 plums altogether.
   What was the average number of plums he sold per day?

---

2. The total mass of 8 onions is 720 g.
   What is their average mass?

---

3. The average of 3 numbers is 12.4.
   Find the sum of the numbers.

---

4. If the average length of 4 pieces of ribbon is 28.5 in.,
   find the total length of the 4 pieces.

5. Fill in the missing numbers.

   (a) 2 L 450 ml × 2 = [　　　] L [　　　] ml

   (b) 2 m 65 cm × 3 = [　　　] m [　　　] cm

   (c) 6 km 250 m × 5 = [　　　] km [　　　] m

   (d) 3 kg 300 g ÷ 3 = [　　　] kg [　　　] g

   (e) 5 h 30 min ÷ 3 = [　　　] h [　　　] min

   (f) 1 L 600 ml ÷ 4 = [　　　] ml

   (g) 4 lb 3 oz × 6 = [　　　] lb [　　　] oz

   (h) 2 ft 10 in. × 4 = [　　　] ft [　　　] in.

6. The total mass of 4 bags of flour is 9 kg 400 g.
   Find their average mass.

7. There are 6 containers. The average amount of water in each
   container is 2 L 250 ml. Find the total amount of water in the
   6 containers.

EXERCISE 3

1. The average mass of Ali, Mick, and Samy is 45 kg.
   Ali and Mick together have a mass of 85 kg.
   Find Samy's mass.

2. Peter spent an average of $4.50 per day from Monday to Saturday.
   He spent $5.20 on Sunday. What was the average amount of money
   he spent per day from Monday to Sunday?

EXERCISE 4

1. The following are measurements of the amount of time it took to do an activity to the nearest twelfth of an hour.

$1\frac{2}{3}$	$1\frac{5}{6}$	$1\frac{1}{2}$	$1\frac{1}{3}$	$1\frac{2}{3}$	$1\frac{2}{3}$
$1\frac{1}{4}$	$1\frac{7}{12}$	$1\frac{3}{4}$	$1\frac{5}{6}$	$1\frac{1}{4}$	$1\frac{5}{12}$

(a) Plot the measurements.

(b) Find the difference between the longest time and the shortest time.

(c) Find the average of the values.

(d) Express the following time in hours and minutes.

    (i)   The longest time

    (ii) The shortest time

    (iii) The most common time

2. Bill measured the length of the bean pods from two different varieties of beans at harvest time to the nearest eighth of an inch and recorded the following results.

Variety 1

$6\frac{1}{2}$	$5\frac{5}{8}$	$6\frac{1}{8}$	$6\frac{1}{8}$	$5\frac{3}{8}$	$6\frac{1}{8}$	$6\frac{1}{8}$	$6\frac{1}{8}$	7	6	$5\frac{5}{8}$	$6\frac{1}{8}$
$6\frac{1}{4}$	$6\frac{1}{4}$	$6\frac{1}{2}$	$5\frac{7}{8}$	$5\frac{7}{8}$	$5\frac{7}{8}$	$5\frac{5}{8}$	$6\frac{3}{4}$	$6\frac{3}{4}$	$6\frac{1}{8}$	6	$6\frac{1}{4}$

Variety 2

$4\frac{3}{4}$	$4\frac{3}{4}$	$4\frac{7}{8}$	$4\frac{7}{8}$	$4\frac{7}{8}$	5	$4\frac{1}{2}$	$4\frac{5}{8}$	$4\frac{1}{4}$	4	$5\frac{1}{4}$	$5\frac{1}{4}$
$4\frac{5}{8}$	$4\frac{1}{2}$	$4\frac{3}{8}$	$4\frac{5}{8}$	$4\frac{5}{8}$	$5\frac{3}{8}$	$5\frac{1}{8}$	4	$4\frac{1}{2}$	$4\frac{7}{8}$	5	$4\frac{5}{8}$

(a) Plot the results.

Which variety had longer pods?

(b) What is the difference in pod length between the longest and shortest in Variety 1?

(c) What is the difference in pod length between the longest and shortest pod in Variety 2?

(d) What is average pod length of Variety 1?

EXERCISE 5

1. Look at the map.

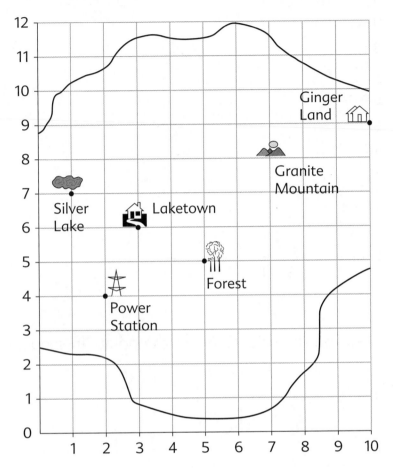

(a) Is Laketown at (6, 3) or at (3, 6)?

(b) Write the coordinates for each of the following places.

Place	Coordinates
Granite Mountain	
Silver Lake	
Forest	
Power Station	

(c) A church is located at coordinates (5, 8).
On the map, graph the location of the church.

(d) Draw a river that starts at (7, 8) and ends at (6, 12).

2. Graph each ordered pair on the grid. Connect the points in sequence.

(a) (4, 1)
(b) (6, 1)
(c) (7, 2)
(d) (3, 2)
(e) (5, 2)
(f) (5, 3)
(g) (3, 4)
(h) (2, 6)
(i) (3, 8)
(j) (5, 9)
(k) (7, 8)
(l) (8, 6)
(m) (7, 4)

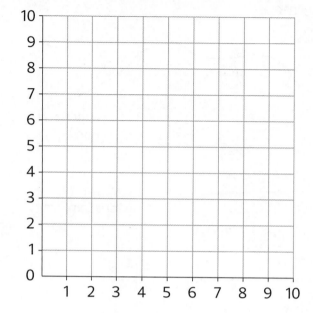

3. Graph each ordered pair on the grid. Connect the points in sequence.

(a) (8, 4)
(b) (8, 5)
(c) (9, 5)
(d) (8, 2)
(e) (3, 2)
(f) (0, 5)
(g) (2, 5)
(h) (3, 4)
(i) (5, 4)
(j) (5, 5)
(k) (7, 5)
(l) (3, 5)
(m) (5, 6)
(n) (8, 6)
(o) (2, 6)
(p) (5, 8)
(q) (7, 8)
(r) (5, 9)

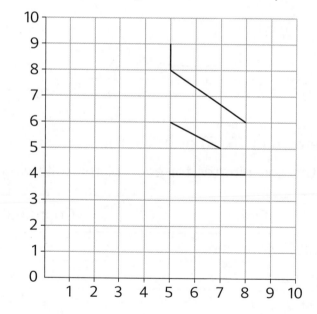

Unit 10: Average, Plots, and Graphs

EXERCISE 6

1. (a) Find the length of each line segment.

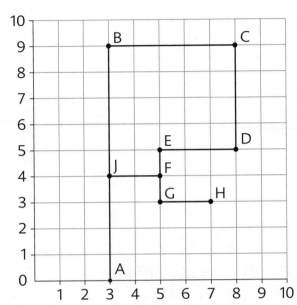

(i) Line BC = [ ] units

(ii) Line EG = [ ] units

(iii) Line AB = [ ] units

(b) To find the length of DE, do you subtract the first or second coordinates in the ordered pairs for points D and E?

[ ]

(c) What is the distance from C to a point at (2, 9)?

[ ]

2. A rectangle has vertices at (4, 2), (4, 10), (10, 10), and (10, 2)? What is its perimeter in units?

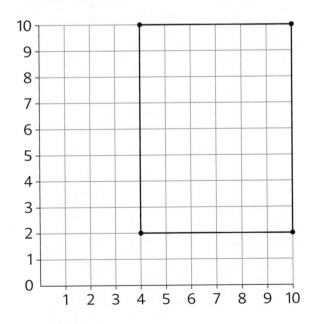

[ ]

3. A polygon has vertices with the coordinates
   (4, 4), (4, 7), (6, 7), (6, 8), (3, 8), (3, 10), (8, 10), and (8, 4).
   What is its perimeter in units?

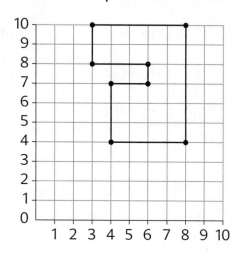

4. Point K is at (12, 7). Point P is 10 units from Point K
   in the vertical direction. What are the coordinates
   of Point P?

5. Square A has sides 6 units long.
   Vertex A is at point (3, 6).

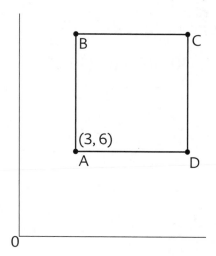

(a) Vertex B is at point [   ].

(b) Vertex C is at point [   ].

(c) Vertex D is at point [   ].

EXERCISE 7

1. (a) Graph the ordered pairs (2, 2), (3, 4), and (4, 6).
Then connect the points.

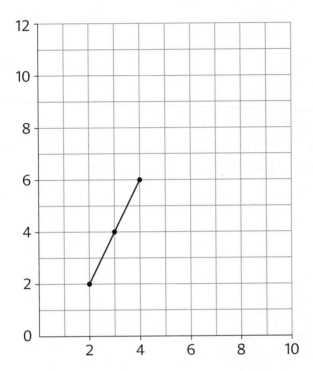

(b) Extend the line.
The following points are on the line.
Complete the coordinates.

(i) (5, ☐)

(ii) (☐ , 10)

(iii) (☐ , 0)

2. (a) Complete the table to show how the perimeter (*p*) of a square changes if the side (*s*) increases in length by 1 unit each time.

s	1	2	3	4
p				

(b) List the ordered pairs (*s*, *p*).

(c) Graph the relationship between the length of the side and perimeter. Connect the points to form a line.

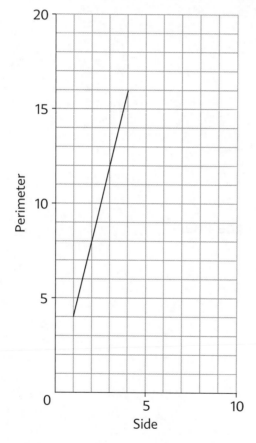

(d) Each time the side increases by 1, the perimeter increases

[   ] times as much.

3. (a) Add 1 to each value *x* to find *y*.
Then complete the table.

x	1	2	3	4	5	6
y	2					
(x, y)	(1, 2)					

(b) Multiply each value of *x* by 2 and then add 1 to find *y*.
Then complete the table.

x	1	2	3	4	5	6
y	3					
(x, y)	(1, 3)					

(c) Graph the ordered pairs and connect the points for each set of values.

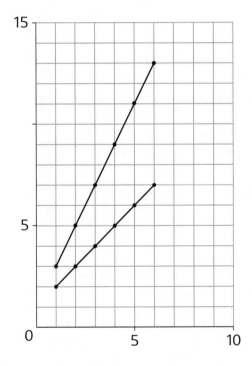

(d) Compare the two lines.

4. Jake bought 18 m of fencing.
The fencing is in 1-m sections.
He wants to find the greatest rectangular area that
he can fence with it.

(a) Complete the table.

Perimeter (m)	P	18	18	18	18	18	18	18	18
Width (m)	w	1	2	3	4	5	6	7	8
Length (m)	l	8							
Area (m²)	A	8							

(b) What is the greatest area that he can fence?

(c) List the ordered pairs for

   (i) (w, P)

   (ii) (w, l)

   (iii) (w, A)

(d) Plot the relationship between the width and the perimeter, length, and area on a single graph.

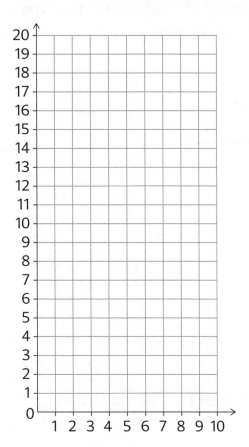

(e) Describe each graph.

EXERCISE 8

1. The line graph shows the enrolment of a school for four years. Study the graph and answer the questions.

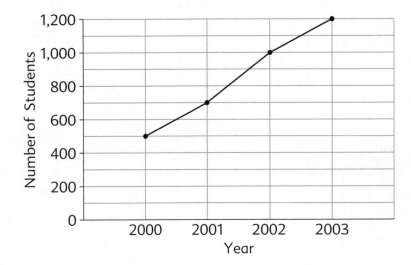

(a) What was the increase in enrolment from 2002 to 2003?

(b) When did the enrolment increase by 300 students in one year?

(c) What was the difference between the enrolment in 2000 and the enrolment in 2003?

(d) What was the total enrolment in the four years?

2. The line graph shows the daily sales of watermelons in a supermarket over a week. Study the graph and answer the questions.

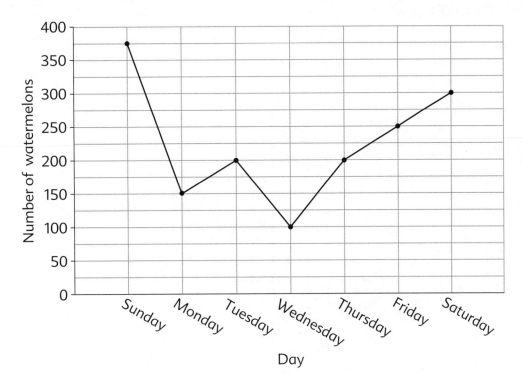

(a) On which day was the sales the lowest?

(b) What were the sales on Sunday?

(c) On which day were 300 watermelons sold?

(d) What was the increase in the sales from Friday to Saturday?

(e) When did the sales decrease by 100 in one day?

3. The line graph shows the height of a plant measured at 8 A.M. every day for five days. Study the graph and answer the questions.

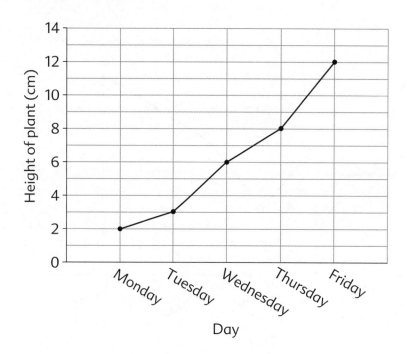

(a) What was the height of the plant measured on Tuesday?

(b) What was the increase in the height of the plant from Thursday to Friday?

(c) When did the plant grow by 3 cm in a day?

(d) When did the plant grow the fastest in a day?
    What was the increase in height?

(e) How many days did the plant take to grow from 2 cm to 12 cm?

4. The line graph shows the number of visitors in a park between 6 A.M. and 10 A.M. on a Sunday morning. Study the graph and answer the questions.

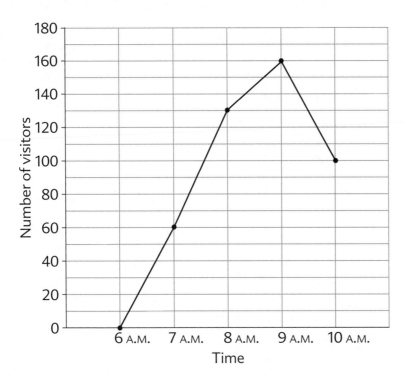

(a) At what time were there 60 visitors in the park?

(b) How many visitors were there in the park at 8 A.M.?

(c) When did the number of visitors increase by 30 in 1 hour?

(d) When did the number of visitors increase the most in 1 hour?

(e) When did the number of visitors decrease by 60 in 1 hour?

5. The line graph shows the exchange rate between Hong Kong dollar and Singapore dollar in a certain year. Study the graph and answer the questions.

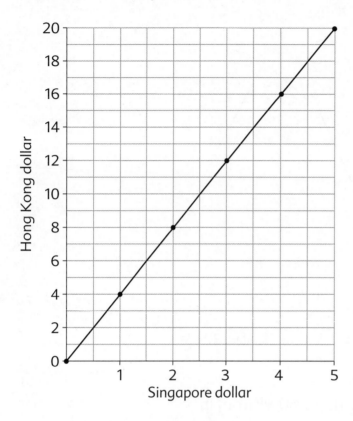

(a) Complete the table.

Singapore dollars	1	2		4	
Hong Kong dollars			12		20

(b) Hong Kong $10 could be exchanged for Singapore $ _____ .

(c) Singapore $4.50 could be exchanged for Hong Kong $ _____ .

(d) How many Singapore dollars could be exchanged for 100 Hong Kong dollars? _____

6. A tap was turned on for 6 minutes to fill a tank with water.
   The line graph shows the volume of water in the tank at the end
   of each minute. Study the graph and answer the questions.

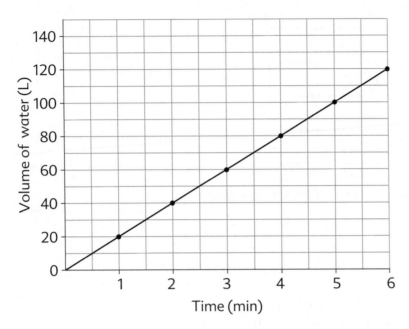

(a) How long did it take to fill the tank with 60 L
    of water?

(b) How long did it take to fill the tank with 90 L
    of water?

(c) How much water was in the tank at the end
    of 2 minutes?

(d) How much water was in the tank at the end
    of $3\frac{1}{2}$ minutes?

(e) Complete the table.

Time (min)	1	2	3	4	5
Volume of water (L)					

REVIEW 10

1. The table shows the savings of 4 children.
   Find the average saving.

Jim	$14.50
Andy	$25.09
Joanna	$36
Angela	$26.41

   [ ]

2. Find the average of each of the following.

   (a) 6.5 L, 0.25 L, 0.08 L, 9.65 L

   [ ]

   (b) 4.8 kg, 15 kg, 11.3 kg, 3.1 kg

   [ ]

3. The average mass of two watermelons is 1.85 kg.
   The mass of one watermelon is 1.26 kg. What is the
   mass of the other watermelon?

   [ ]

4. The total cost of 4 kg of prawns and 3 kg of fish
   is $76.50. If 1 kg of prawns costs $12.75, find the
   cost of 1 kg of fish.

   [ ]

5. Fill in the missing numbers.

   (a) 2 yd 2 ft × 5 = [ ] yd [ ] ft

   (b) 6 gal 3 qt × 6 = [ ] gal [ ] qt

   (c) 5 qt 2 c × 7 = [ ] qt [ ] c

   (d) 6 qt 1 pt × 4 = [ ] qt [ ] pt

   (e) 5 lb 12 oz ÷ 4 = [ ] lb [ ] oz

   (f) 3 ft 8 in. ÷ 11 = [ ] ft [ ] in.

   (g) 7 gal 2 qt ÷ 6 = [ ] gal [ ] qt

6. Mitchell jogged 2.2 mi on Friday.
   He jogged 0.7 mi less on Saturday than on Friday.

   (a) Find the total distance he jogged on the two days.

   (b) What was the average distance he jogged per day?

7. A rectangle has coordinates at (3, 2), (3, 5), (7, 2),
   and (7, 5) on a grid with 1-cm squares.
   Find the area of the rectangle.

8. The total length of 4 ribbons is 9 m 40 cm.
   Find the average length.

9. Fill in the missing number.
   The average of 64, 73, 58, [   ], and 70
   is 62.4.

10. Betsy traveled 8,740 km in 4 months.
    What was the average distance she traveled
    per month?

11. Anabelle and her three friends bought lunch together.
    They spent an average of $8.25 each.
    What was the total cost of the lunch?

12. The graph shows the weekly sales of tickets at the zoo during a school break. Study the graph and fill in the boxes.

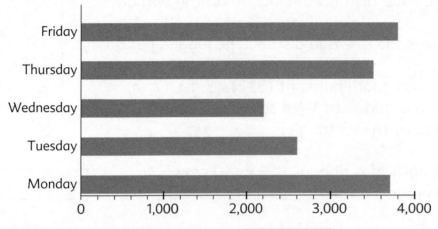

(a) Most tickets were sold on _____.

(b) The increase in sales of the tickets from Wednesday to Friday was _____.

(c) The overall sales over the five days were _____.

(d) The average sales per day were _____.

13. The graph shows the sale of books from January to June.

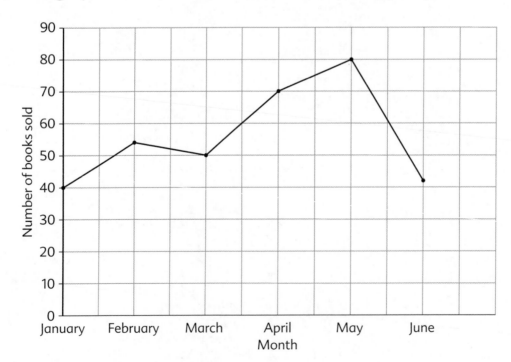

(a) Find the average number of books sold each month.

(b) What was the decrease in the number of books sold between May and June?

(c) If 1 book costs $4.25, how much was the sale in February?

14. A tap was turned on to fill a tank with water to its brim. The line graph shows the volume of water in the tank at regular intervals of time.

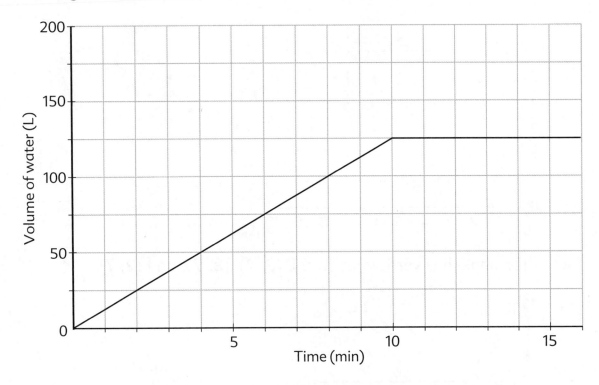

(a) What was the volume of water in the tank when it was full?

(b) How long did it take to fill the tank to its brim?

15. Graph each ordered pair on the grid. Connect the points.

(a) (2, 5)   (b) (3, 6)   (c) (4, 7)   (d) (5, 8)

(e) (6, 7)   (f) (7, 6)   (g) (8, 5)   (h) (7, 4)

(i) (6, 3)   (j) (5, 2)   (k) (4, 3)   (l) (3, 4)

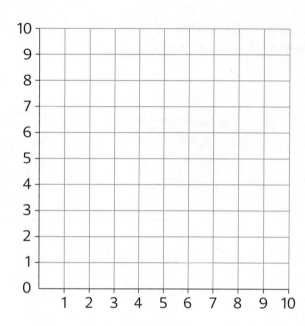

16. A rectangle has vertices at (2, 2), (8, 2), (8, 7), and (2, 7).

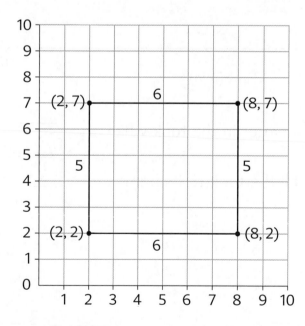

What is the perimeter of the rectangle in units?

17. Sam took a 6-hour bicycle trip.
    He traveled 117 mi in all.
    What was his average speed in miles per hour?

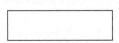

18. Graph the ordered pairs (1, 3) and (6, 8).
    Then connect the two points.

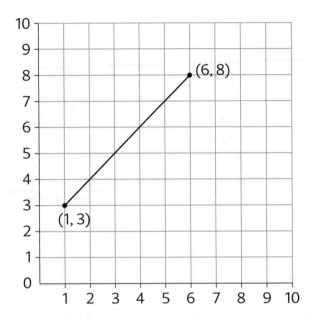

The following points are on the line. Complete the coordinates.

(a) (2, ☐)

(b) (☐, 5)

(c) (4, ☐)

EXERCISE 1

1. What is the size of each angle in degrees?

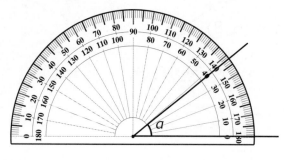

m∠a = [ ]

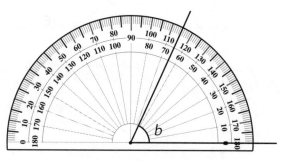

m∠b = [ ]

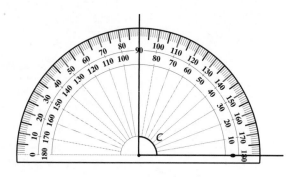

m∠c = [ ]

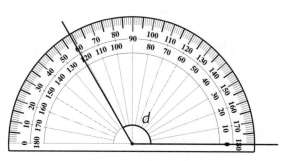

m∠d = [ ]

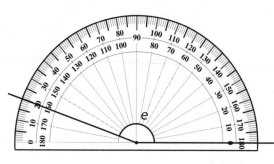

m∠e = [ ]

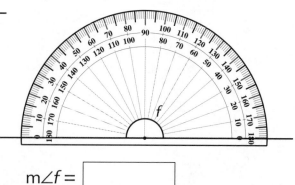

m∠f = [ ]

Unit 11: Angles, Triangles, and Quadrilaterals

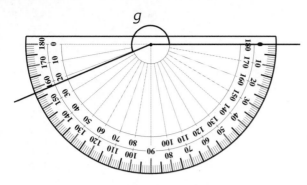

m∠g = [   ]

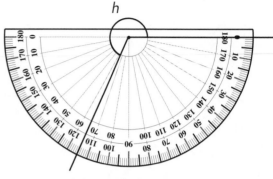

m∠h = [   ]

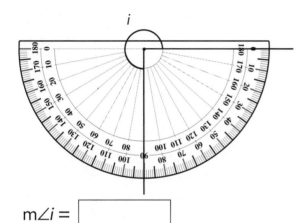

m∠i = [   ]

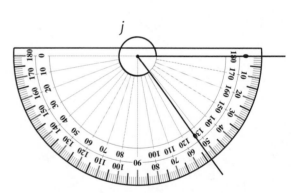

m∠j = [   ]

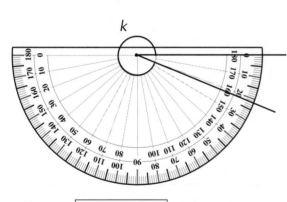

m∠k = [   ]

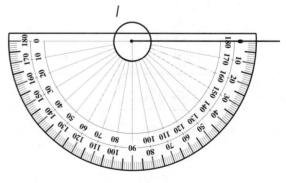

m∠l = [   ]

2. Complete the table.

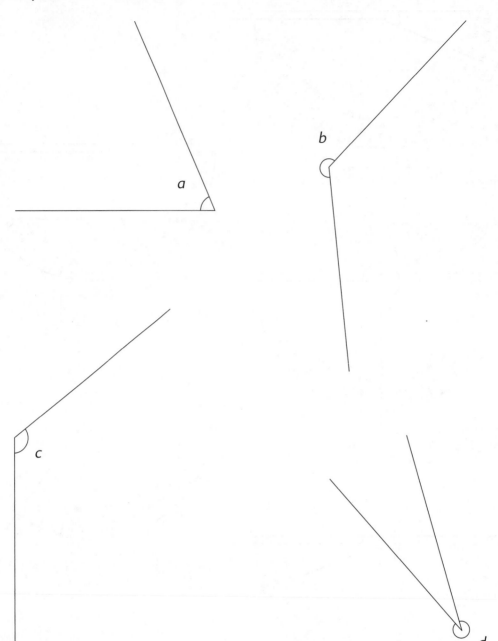

Angle	*a*	*b*	*c*	*d*
Estimate				
Measure				

3. Draw an angle equal to 165°.

4. Draw an angle equal to 250°.

5. Draw an angle equal to 325°.

EXERCISE 2

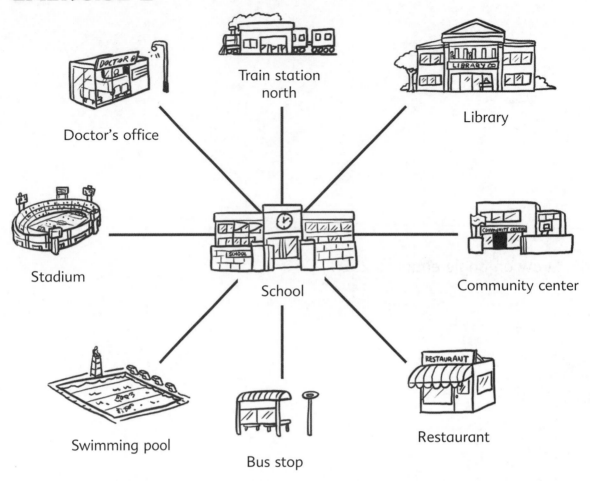

Train station north

Doctor's office

Library

Stadium

School

Community center

Swimming pool

Bus stop

Restaurant

1. In which direction is each place from the school?
    Complete the table.

Place	Direction from School
Train station	north
Bus stop	
Library	
Restaurant	
Stadium	
Doctor's office	
Community center	
Swimming pool	

Unit 11: Angles, Triangles, and Quadrilaterals

2.

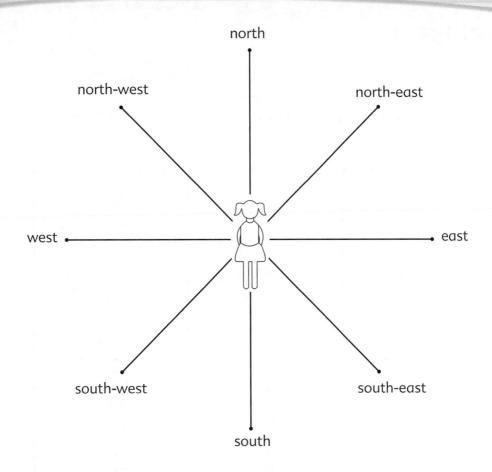

Complete the table.

I am facing	If I turn	I will be facing
north	45° clockwise	
south	90° counterclockwise	
north-west	180° clockwise	
east	135° counterclockwise	
south-east	_____ clockwise	south
north-east	_____ clockwise	south-east
south-east	_____ counterclockwise	north
west	_____ clockwise	north-west

EXERCISE 3

1. Measure the angles and sides of the following triangles.
    Mark equal sides and right angles.
    Then put a (✓) in each equilateral triangle and a (✗) in
    each right triangle.

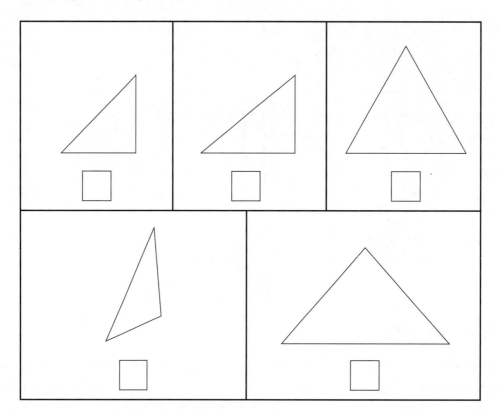

(a) What do you notice about the angles in an

    (i)   isosceles triangle?

    (ii) equilateral triangle?

2. Measure the angles and sides of the following quadrilaterals.
   Mark equal sides, right angles, and parallel sides.
   Then fill in the table with **Yes** or **No**.

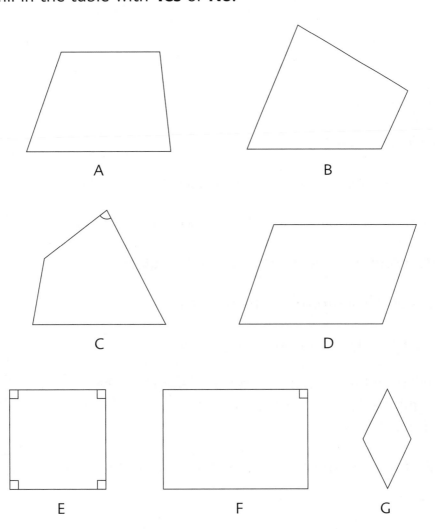

Quadrilateral	Parallelogram	Trapezoid	Rectangle	Square	Rhombus
A					
B					
C					
D					
E					
F					
G					

3. The rhombus is divided into two parts as shown.
   What kind of triangle is each part?

4. Write **True** or **False**.

   (a) All equilateral triangles are isosceles triangles.

   (b) A right triangle cannot be an isosceles triangle.

   (c) A rhombus must have two right angles.

   (d) All parallelograms are rectangles.

   (e) All rectangles are parallelograms.

   (f) When all four angles in a parallelogram are
       right angles and all the sides are of equal length,
       it is a square.

   (g) A trapezoid must have two pairs of parallel sides.

Unit 11: Angles, Triangles, and Quadrilaterals

EXERCISE 4

1. The following figures are not drawn to scale.
   Find the unknown marked angles.

<table>
<tr>
<td>

(a)

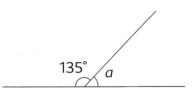

135° a

m∠a =

</td>
<td>

(b)

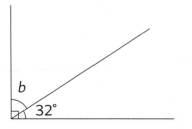

b 32°

m∠b =

</td>
</tr>
<tr>
<td>

(c)

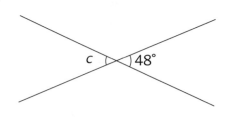

c 48°

m∠c =

</td>
<td>

(d)

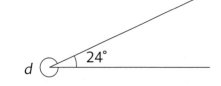

24°
d

m∠d =

</td>
</tr>
<tr>
<td>

(e)

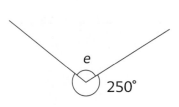

e
250°

m∠e =

</td>
<td>

(f)

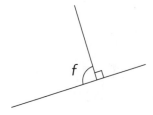

f

m∠f =

</td>
</tr>
<tr>
<td>

(g)

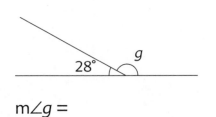

28° g

m∠g =

</td>
<td>

(h)

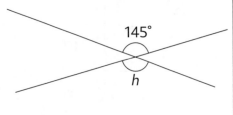

145°
h

m∠h =

</td>
</tr>
</table>

2. The following figures are not drawn to scale.
   Find the unknown marked angles.

(a)

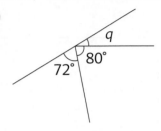

(b)

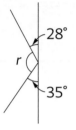

(c)

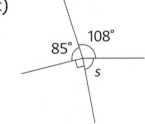

(d)

(e)

EXERCISE 5

1. The following figures are not drawn to scale.
   Find the measure of the angles.

(a) Find m∠ACB.

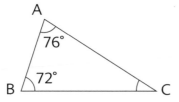

(b) Find m∠TRS.

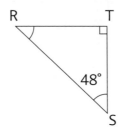

(c) Find m∠LMK.

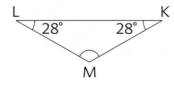

(d) Find m∠FGH.

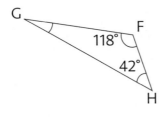

EXERCISE 6

1. The following figures are not drawn to scale.
   Find the unknown marked angles.
   Then check (✓) the right-angled triangles.

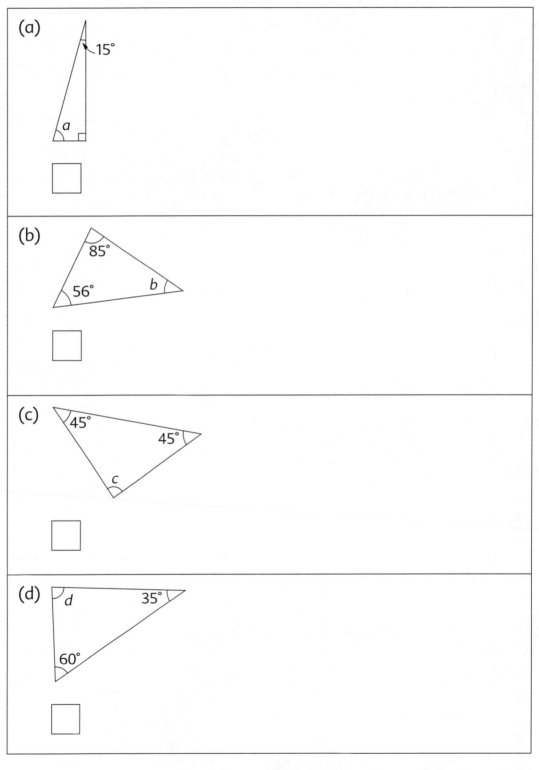

(a)

15°

a

(b)

85°

56°

b

(c)

45°

45°

c

(d)

d

35°

60°

EXERCISE 7

1. The following figures are not drawn to scale.
   Find the measure of the angles.

(a) DBC is a straight line.
    Find m∠ABD.

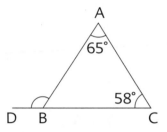

(b) WXY is a straight line.
    Find m∠WXZ.

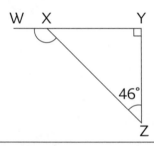

(c) ABD is a straight line.
    Find m∠BDC.

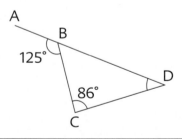

(d) STU is a straight line.
    Find m∠SRT.

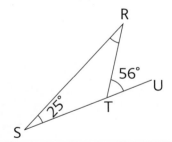

EXERCISE 8

1. The following figures are not drawn to scale.
    Find the unknown marked angles.
    Then check (✔) the isosceles triangles.

(a)

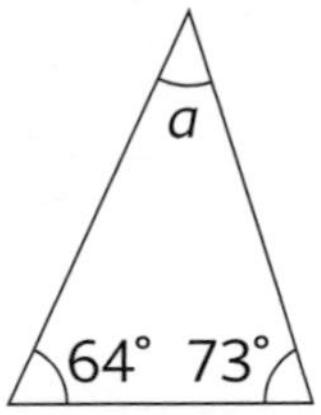

64° 73° a

☐

(b)

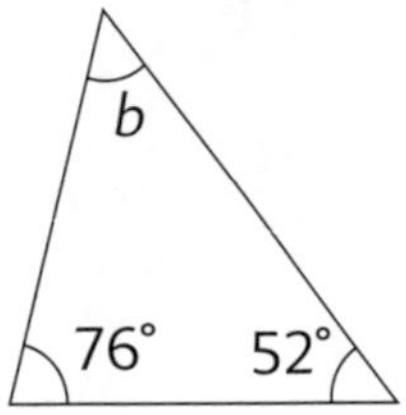

b 76°   52°

☐

(c)

35°   35° c

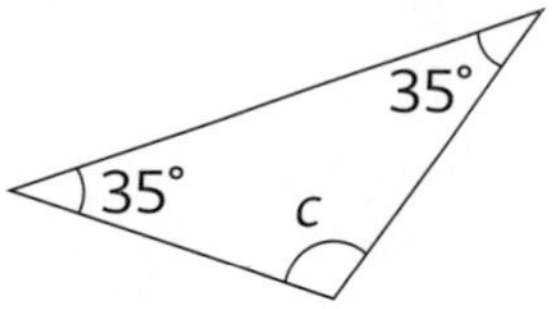

☐

(d)

47° d

☐

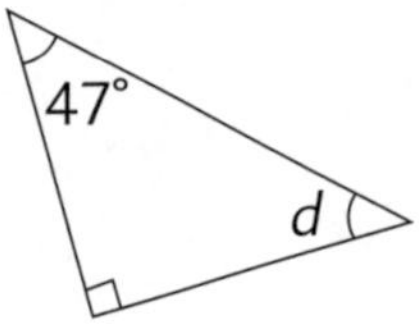

2. The following figures are not drawn to scale.
    Find the unknown marked angles.
    Then check (✓) the equilateral triangles.

(a)

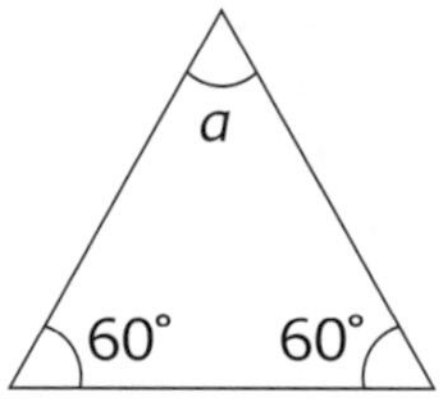

a

60°   60°

☐

(b)

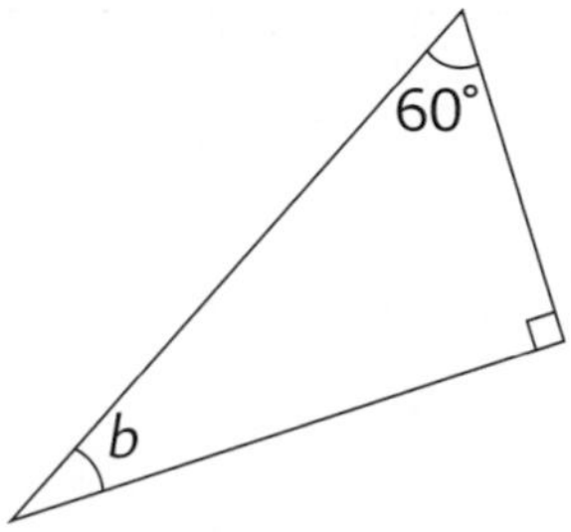

60°

b

☐

(c)

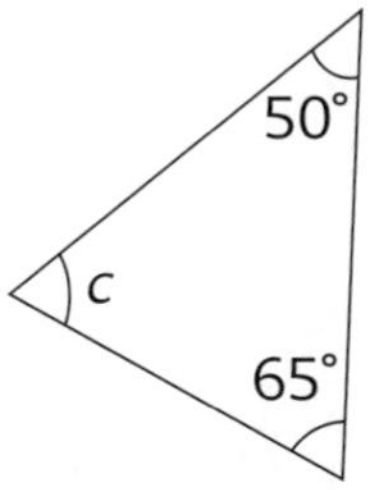

50°

c

65°

☐

(d)

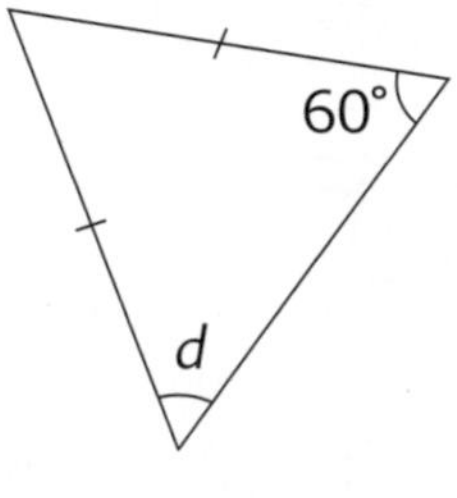

60°

d

☐

EXERCISE 9

1. The following figures are not drawn to scale.
   Find the unknown marked angles.

(a)

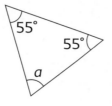

(b)

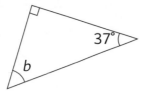

(c) BCD is a straight line.

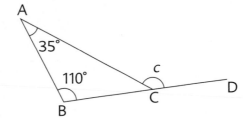

(d)

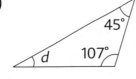

(e) ACD is a straight line.

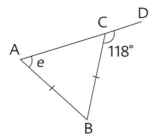

(f) ABC is a straight line.

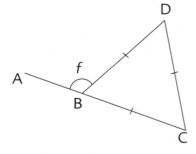

(g) DCB is a straight line.

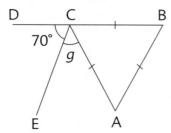

(h) BCD is a straight line.

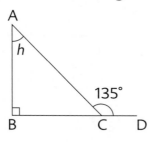

EXERCISE 10

1. The following figures are not drawn to scale.
   Find the unknown marked angles.

(a)

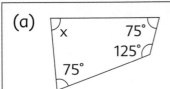

(b)

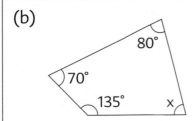

(c)

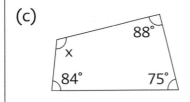

(d)

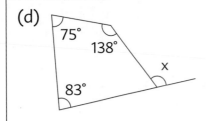

(e)

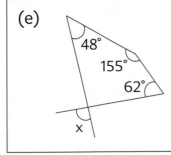

EXERCISE 11

1. The following parallelograms are not drawn to scale.
   Find the unknown marked angles.

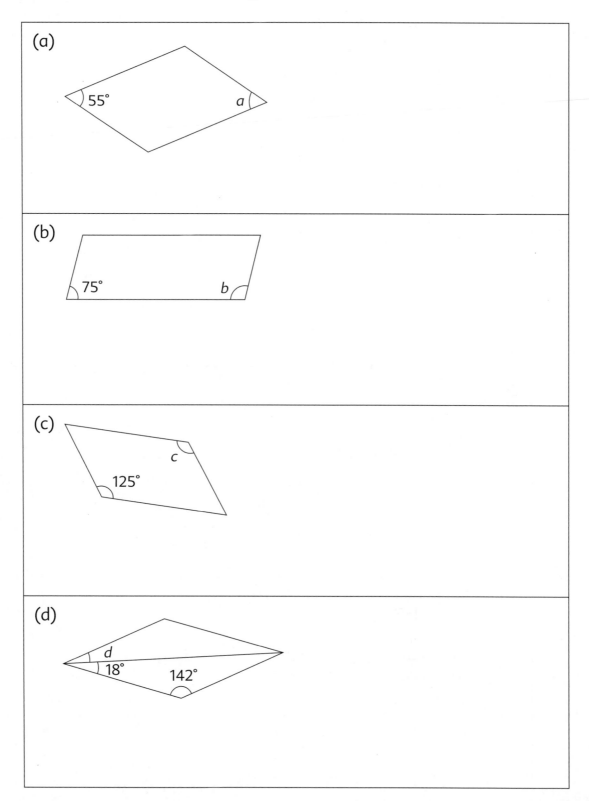

(a)

55°

a

(b)

75°

b

(c)

c

125°

(d)

d

18°

142°

(e)

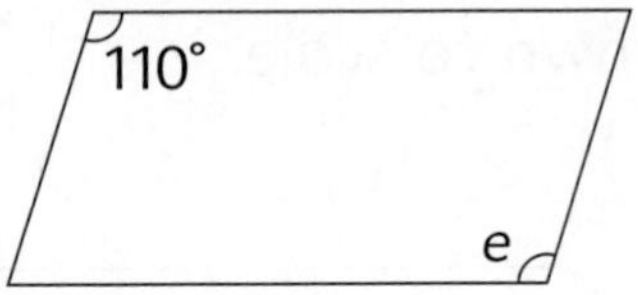

110°

e

(f)

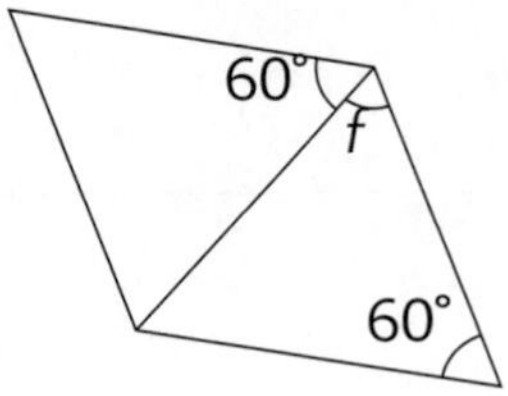

60°

f

60°

(g)

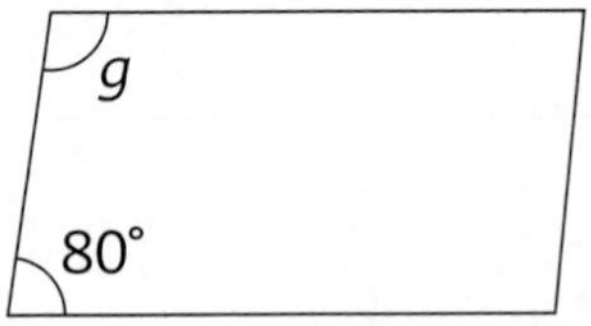

g

80°

(h)

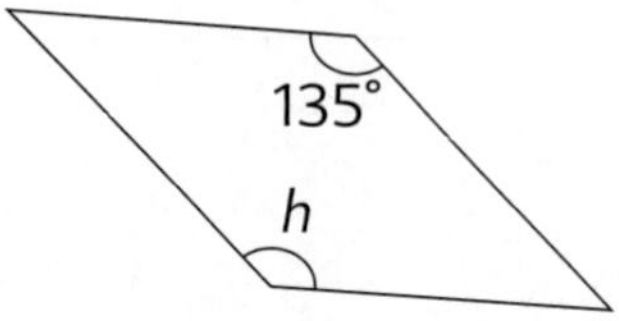

135°

h

EXERCISE 12

1. The following rectangles are not drawn to scale.
   Find the measure of the angles in each rectangle.

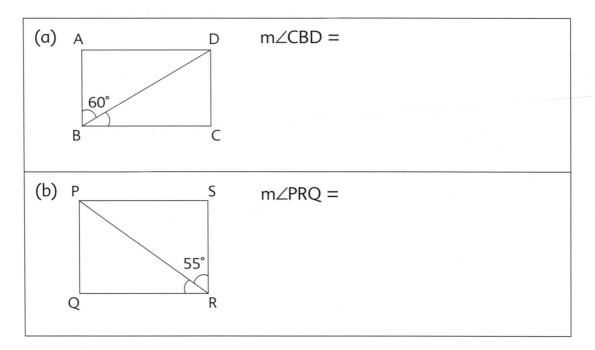

(a) m∠CBD =

(b) m∠PRQ =

2. The following rhombuses are not drawn to scale.
   Find the unknown marked angles.

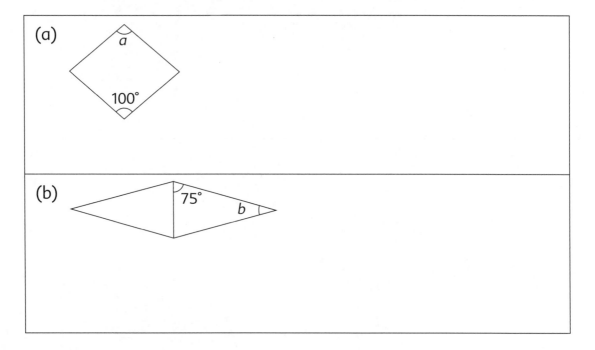

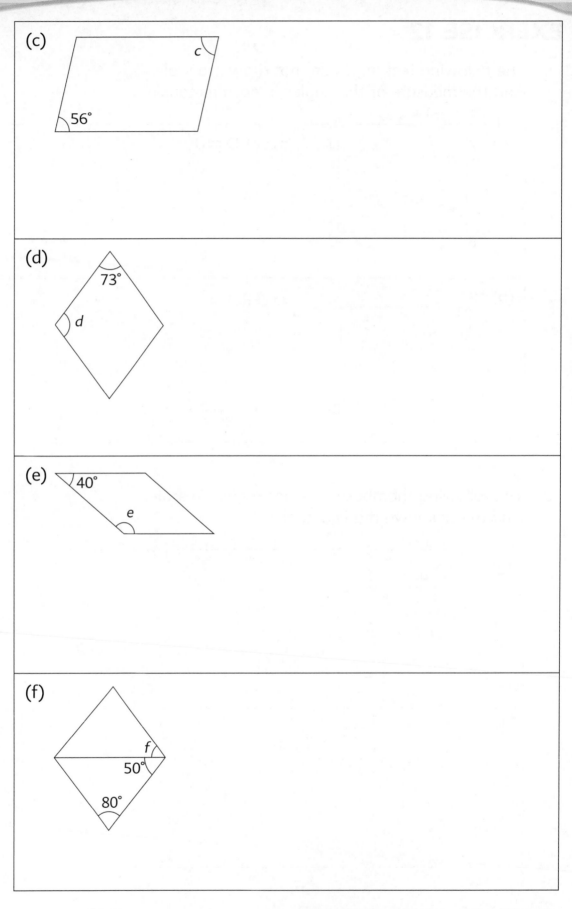

(c)

56°   c

(d)

73°
d

(e)

40°
e

(f)

f
50°
80°

3. The following trapezoids are not drawn to scale.
   Find the unknown marked angles.

(a)

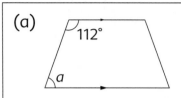

(b)

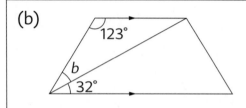

(c)

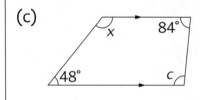

(d)

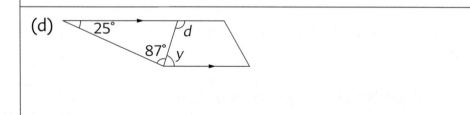

REVIEW 11

1. Which of the following angles is an acute angle?

A

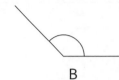

B

C

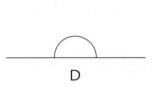

D

[ ]

2. Write **True** or **False**.

(a) All four sides of a rhombus are equal. [ ]

(b) Acute angles are more than 90°. [ ]

(c) Opposite sides of a parallelogram are equal. [ ]

(d) Only two angles of an equilateral triangle are equal. [ ]

(e) Only one pair of opposite sides of a trapezoid is parallel. [ ]

(f) Sum of all three angles of a triangle is 180°. [ ]

(g) A rectangle is a parallelogram with four right angles. [ ]

(h) Each side in an isosceles triangle is different. [ ]

3. Look at the figures and answer the following questions.

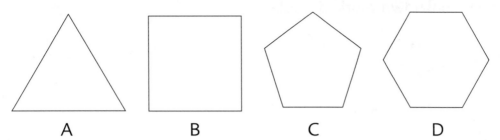

| A | B | C | D |

(a) Which is a quadrilateral? ☐

(b) Which is a pentagon? ☐

(c) Which is a hexagon? ☐

4. Name the following triangles.

(a)

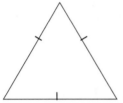

☐

(b)

☐

5. Divide an equilateral triangle into two parts as shown.
   What kind of triangle is each part?

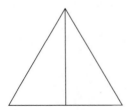

☐

6. The following quadrilaterals are not drawn to scale.
   Find the unknown marked angles.

   (a)

   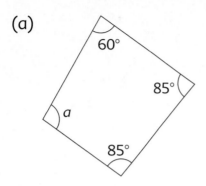

   (b)

   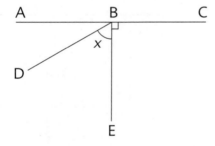

7. The figure is not drawn to scale.
   m∠ABD = 61°. Find m∠x.

   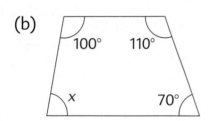

8. The following figures are not drawn to scale.
   Find the unknown marked angles.

   (a) ACD is a straight line.

   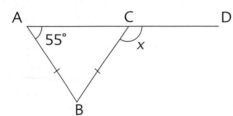

(b) ABC is a straight line.

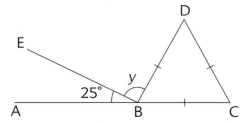

(c) ABC is a straight line.

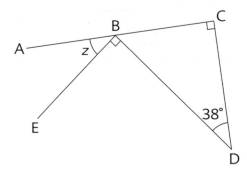

9. The figure is not drawn to scale. ABCD is a parallelogram, BCE is a straight line, and m∠BAD = 108°. Find m∠DCE.

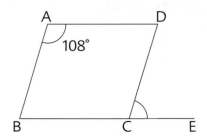

10. The figure is not drawn to scale. PQRS is a parallelogram, RT ⊥ PS, and m∠PQR = 55°. Find m∠TRS.

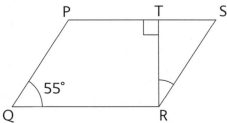

11. The figure is not drawn to scale.
    Find the unknown marked angle.

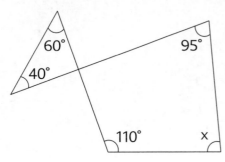

12. The figure is not drawn to scale. ABC and BDC
    are right-angled triangles, m∠ACD = 35°, and
    m∠DBC = 40°. Find m∠BAC.

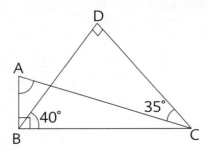

13. The figure is not drawn to scale. PQRS is a trapezoid,
    TR = TS, and m∠RST = 74°. Find m∠QRT.

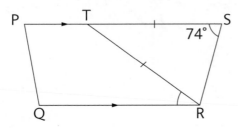

14. The rhombus is not drawn to scale.
    Find the unknown marked angle.

15. The rhombus is not drawn to scale.
    Find the unknown marked angle.

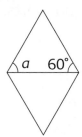

[   ]

16. BCD is an isosceles triangle.
    ABC and EBD are straight lines.
    Find m∠BDC.

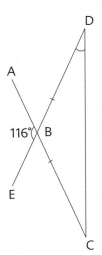

[   ]

17. In trapezoid ABCD, AD // BC.
    Find m∠ABC and m∠DCB.

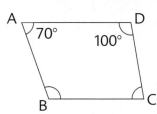

(a) m∠ABC = [   ]

(b) m∠DCB = [   ]

EXERCISE 1

1. In each of the following, the whole is divided into 100 equal parts. What percentage of the whole is shaded?

(a)

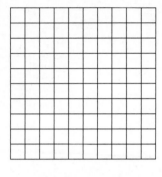

[ ] %

(b)

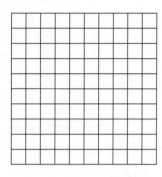

[ ] %

(c)

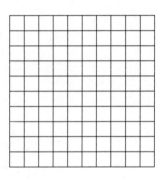

[ ] %

(d)

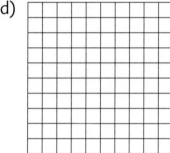

[ ] %

(e)

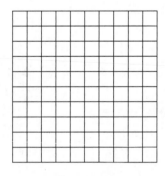

[ ] %

(f)

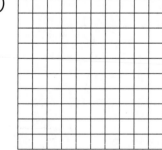

[ ] %

2. In each of the following, the whole is divided into 100 equal parts.

   (a) Shade 80% of the whole.   (b) Shade 63% of the whole.

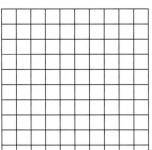   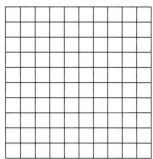

3. Express each fraction as a percentage.

(a) $\frac{87}{100}$ =	(b) $\frac{5}{100}$ = 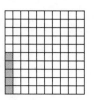
(c) $\frac{16}{100}$ =	(d) $\frac{71}{100}$ =
(e) $\frac{68}{100}$ =	(f) $\frac{50}{100}$ =
(g) $\frac{99}{100}$ =	(h) $\frac{100}{100}$ =

4. Fill in the missing numbers.

   (a) $7\% = \frac{\square}{100}$

   (b) $1\% = \frac{\square}{100}$

   (c) $43\% = \frac{\square}{100}$

   (d) $99\% = \frac{\square}{100}$

   (e) $14\% = \frac{14}{\square}$

   (f) $68\% = \frac{68}{\square}$

   (g) $5\% = \frac{5}{\square}$

   (h) $84\% = \frac{84}{\square}$

EXERCISE 2

1. Express each decimal as a percentage.

(a) 0.15 =	(b) 0.86 =
(c) 0.4 =	(d) 0.9 =
(e) 0.47 =	(f) 0.12 =
(g) 0.04 =	(h) 0.5 =
(i) 0.75 =	(j) 0.06 =

2. Express each percentage as a decimal.

(a) 24% =	(b) 37% =
(c) 78% =	(d) 6% =
(e) 62% =	(f) 53% =
(g) 10% =	(h) 7% =
(i) 80% =	(j) 90% =

3. Express each percentage as a fraction in its simplest form.

(a) $22\% = \dfrac{22}{100}$ $=$	(b) $45\% =$
(c) $96\% =$	(d) $52\% =$
(e) $6\% =$	(f) $40\% =$
(g) $90\% =$	(h) $8\% =$
(i) $75\% =$	(j) $50\% =$

EXERCISE 3

1. Express each fraction as a percentage.

(a) $\frac{1}{2} =$	(b) $\frac{9}{50} =$
(c) $\frac{17}{20} =$	(d) $\frac{12}{25} =$
(e) $\frac{3}{5} =$	(f) $\frac{9}{15} =$
(g) $\frac{8}{50} =$	(h) $\frac{3}{12} =$
(i) $\frac{18}{75} =$	(j) $\frac{12}{40} =$

2. Express each of the following as a percentage.

(a) 8 out of 40

$$\frac{8}{40} = \frac{2}{10}$$

=

(b) 40 out of 80

(c) 15 out of 50

(d) 7 out of 20

(e) 24 out of 40

EXERCISE 4

1. Express each of the following as a percentage.

(a) 186 out of 200 $\dfrac{186}{200} = \dfrac{93}{100}$ $=$
(b) 39 out of 300
(c) 96 out of 400
(d) 235 out of 500
(e) 122 out of 200

2. Sara mailed 20 Christmas cards. Of them, 9 were mailed to Canada. What percentage of the cards were mailed to Canada?

3. There are 80 members in a school band. Of them, 24 are 6th grade students. What percentage of the members are 6th grade students?

4. There are 200 units in an apartment complex. Of them, 64 are three-bedroom apartments. What percentage of the apartments are three-bedroom apartments?

EXERCISE 5

1. Jane made 50 cookies and 24 of them were chocolate cookies.
    The rest were sugar cookies.

    (a) What percentage of the cookies were chocolate cookies?

    (b) What percentage of the cookies were sugar cookies?

---

2. Ryan had $80. He spent $32 on a book.

    (a) What percentage of his money did he spend on the book?

    (b) What percentage of his money did he have left?

3. There are 400 seats in a concert hall and 120 of them are occupied.

   (a) What percentage of the seats are occupied?

   (b) What percentage of the seats are not occupied?

---

4. The number of swimmers taking part in a swimming competition is 125. Of them, 85 are females.

   (a) What percentage of the swimmers are females?

   (b) What percentage of the swimmers are males?

EXERCISE 6

1. Find the value of each of the following.

(a) 4% of 300	(b) 72% of 15
(c) 30% of $94	(d) 5% of $250
(e) 25% of 240 m	(f) 80% of 25 kg

2. Molly paid $85 last month for her utilities. She spent 55% of this amount on electricity. How much did Molly pay for electricity?

---

3. There were 48 traffic accidents in May last year. Of them, 25% happened on the freeways. How many accidents happened on the freeways?

---

4. Stephanie earns $750 a month. She gives 30% of the money to charity. How much money does Stephanie give to charity?

EXERCISE 7

1. There are 55 apples in a box. Of them, 40% are red apples and the rest are green apples. How many green apples are there in the box?

2. Jordon had $840. He gave 30% of the money to his parents. How much money did he have left for himself?

3. Mike earns $1,200 a month. He saves 15% of the money and spends the rest. How much does he spend each month?

4. There were 750 questions in a mathematics book. Sam answered 82% of them correctly. How many questions did he answer incorrectly?

EXERCISE 8

1. Kate has $1,800 in a savings bank. The bank pays 6% interest per year.

   (a) How much interest will she earn after 1 year?

   (b) How much money will she have in the bank after 1 year?

2. Alicia borrows $2,800 from a bank. The bank charges 8% interest per year. If she pays off the loan in 1 year, how much does she have to pay?

3. The usual price of a clock was $60. At a sale, it was sold at a discount of 20%.

   (a) How much was the discount?

   (b) Find the selling price of the clock.

4. The usual price of a photo album was $15. It was sold at a discount of 25%. Find the selling price of the photo album.

5. A man rents a room for $300 a month. If the rent is increased by 12%, how much more does he have to pay each month?

---

6. A factory had 1,500 workers last year. This year, the number of workers increased by 4%. Find the number of workers after the increase.

REVIEW 12

1. Express 7% as a decimal.

2. Express each fraction as a percentage.
   (a) $\frac{48}{100}$

   (b) $\frac{2}{10}$

   (c) $\frac{5}{500}$

   (d) $\frac{84}{700}$

3. Express each decimal as a percentage.
   (a) 0.57

   (b) 0.25

   (c) 0.15

   (d) 0.03

4. Express each percentage as a fraction in its simplest form.
   (a) 75%

   (b) 25%

   (c) 6%

   (d) 40%

5. Complete the table.

Decimals	0.5	0.8			0.48
Fractions	$\frac{1}{2}$		$\frac{3}{4}$		
Percentage	50%			35%	

6. The membership fee of a club was $5 last year. It was increased by 20% this year. Find the new membership fee.

7. In a group of 20 children, 7 of them wear glasses.

   (a) What percentage of the children wear glasses?

   (b) What percentage of the children do not wear glasses?

8. What percentage of $2 is 80 cents?

9. Find the value of each of the following.

   (a) 10% of $250

   (b) 75% of $1,400

10. Hillary had $240. She spent 35% of the money. How much money did she have left?

11. A vase cost $160. It was sold at 15% above the cost price. Find the selling price.

12. Gary has $12. He spent 25% of the money on food and 20% of it on transport. How much money did he have left?

13. Mary had $50. She spent 20% of the money on a book and 15% of the remainder on a magazine.

    (a) Find the cost of the book.

    (b) Find the cost of the magazine.

14. A school auditorium has 200 seats and 156 of them are occupied. What percentage of the seats are occupied?

15. Sarah saved 15% of her allowance.
    What fraction of her allowance did she save?

16. A library has 1,200 books and 780 books are
    for children. The rest are for adults. What
    percentage of the books are for adults?

17. Mrs. Armand bought a painting for $450 and
    sold it at a profit of 12%. What was the
    selling price?

18. There are 90 children in a school choir and 36
    of them are girls. What percentage of the
    children are boys?

19. In a 500 g bag of mixed nuts, 200 g are
    cashew nuts. What percentage of the mixed
    nuts are not cashew nuts?

20. A store owner bought 50 bicycles for $7,000.
    He sold all of them at a profit of 35%.
    How much profit did he make from each bicycle?

21. In a club, there are 30 girls and 10 boys.
    What percentage of the children are boys?

22. The cost price of a refrigerator is $800. It is
    sold at a discount of 15%. Find the selling price.

EXERCISE 1

1. Find the rate for each of the following.

(a) Jerome pays $225 to rent a hotel room for 3 days.

$$\text{Rate} = \frac{225}{3}$$

$$=$$

The rate is $_____ per day.

(b) Steve types 750 words in 15 minutes.

Rate =

The rate is _____ words per minute.

(c) A machine fills 240 similar jars with jam in 20 minutes.

Rate =

The rate is _____ jars per minute.

(d) A motorcycle can travel a distance of 102 mi on 3 gal of gas.

Rate =

The rate is _____ mi per gallon.

---

2. Fill in the missing numbers.

(a) A machine makes 45 similar cakes per minute.

At this rate, it will make _____ similar cakes in 5 minutes.

(b) Carpets are sold at $225 per m².

At this rate, a similar carpet of area 35 m² will cost

$_____.

(c) Ben lays 25 bricks per hour.

At this rate, Ben will lay _____ bricks of the same kind in 7 hours.

(d) Matthew's family uses 24 m³ of water per month.

At this rate, Matthew's family will use _____ m³ of water in 6 months.

EXERCISE 2

1. There are 2,000 words on a page. How long will Alice take to read the page if she reads at the rate of 100 words per minute?

_____

2. The room rate of Sunshine Hotel is $80 per day. At this rate, how many days did Ben stay at the hotel if he paid $400?

_____

3. A wheel makes 6 revolutions per minute. At this rate, how long will it take to make 45 revolutions?

4. The workers in a factory were paid at the rate of $6 per hour. Justin worked for 7 hours. How much was he paid?

---

5. A machine can make 200 similar loaves of bread per minute. At this rate, how many similar loaves of bread can the machine make in 5 minutes?

---

6. A car can travel 12 km on 1 L of gas. At this rate, how much gas will be used if the car travels a distance of 180 km?

EXERCISE 3

1. A taxi driver earns $300 in 5 days.

   The rate is $ ☐ per day.

   (a) At this rate, he will earn $ ☐ in 6 days.

   (b) He will take ☐ days to earn $1,200.

2. A car travels 84 km on 6 L of gas.

   The rate is ☐ km per liter.

   (a) At this rate, it can travel ☐ km on 16 L of gas.

   (b) It can travel 210 km on ☐ L of gas.

3. The cost of cementing a courtyard of area 40 m^2 is $1,600.

   The rate is $ ☐ per m^2.

   (a) At this rate, the cost of cementing an area of 90 m^2 is $ ☐ .

   (b) The cost of cementing an area of ☐ m^2 is $2,000.

4. A printing machine can roll out 600 identical pages of printed material in 4 minutes.

   The rate is ☐ pages per minute.

   (a) At this rate, the machine can roll out ☐ identical pages in 15 minutes.

   (b) It will take the machine ☐ minutes to roll out 750 identical pages.

5. A watch loses time at a rate of 80 seconds in 2 days.

   (a) How many seconds will it lose in 3 days?

   (b) How long will it take to lose 200 seconds?

---

6. A machine can bind 1,500 similar books in 12 minutes.

   (a) How many such books can it bind in 5 minutes?

   (b) How long will it take to bind 1,000 such books?

EXERCISE 4

1. The table shows the rates of charges for renting bicycles.

First hour	$3
Every additional hour	$2

(a) Jacob rented a bicycle for 2 hours. How much should he pay?

(b) Jackie rented a bicycle from 2:00 p.m. to 6:00 p.m. How much should she pay?

(c) Four boys rented 2 bicycles for 3 hours. If they shared the cost equally, how much should each boy pay?

2. The table shows the rates of charges for water consumption in a month.

First 20 m³	$0.56 per m³
Next 20 m³	$0.80 per m³
Additional amount above 40 m³	$1.17 per m³

(a) What is the charge for 15 m³ of water used in a month?

(b) What is the charge for 30 m³ of water used in a month?

(c) What is the charge for 45 m³ of water used in a month?

REVIEW 13

1. The cost of 8 apples is $2.50.
    Find the cost of 20 such apples.

    ☐

2. Fill in the missing numbers.

    (a) A tailor sews 24 bags in a day.

    At this rate, he can make ☐ of such bags in 8 days.

    (b) A car travels 124 km on 8 L of gas.

    The rate is ☐ km per L.

    At this rate, it can travel ☐ km on 20 L of gas.

    (c) The cost of tiling a floor of area 60m² is $2,400.

    The rate is $ ☐ per m².

    The cost of tiling ☐ m² is $4,000.

3. Fill in the missing numbers.

    (a) A car drove 240 m in 4 hours.

    The rate is ☐ mph.

    (b) (i) A painter paints 320 sq ft of wall in 8 hours.
            How much can he paint in an hour?

    ☐

    (ii) At this rate, he will take ☐ hours to
         paint 2,000 sq ft.

    (c) One pipe can fill a tank in 5.5 hours.

    At this rate, it will take ☐ hours
    to fill 4 tanks.

4. Jim traveled 495 miles at 55 mph.
    How long did the trip take?

    ☐

5. A worker can make 288 baskets in 3 days.
    What is the rate per hour?

    ☐

6. An empty rectangular tank measures 60 cm by 50 cm by 24 cm. It is to be filled with water from a tap.

   (a) If the water flows from the tap at the rate of 12 L per minute, how long will it take to fill up the tank? (1 liter = 1,000 cm³)

       ☐

   (b) If the tank is leaking at the rate of 4 L per minute, how much time will it take to fill up the tank with the same tap as in (a)?

       ☐

7. A watch gains time at the rate of 75 seconds in 2 days.

   (a) How much time will it gain in 6 days?

       ☐

   (b) How long will it take to gain 600 seconds?

       ☐

8. The table shows the taxi fares in a city.

First 1.5 km	$3.20
For every additional 100 m	$0.15
Waiting charge for every 15 mins	$1.00

   (a) Find the taxi fare for a journey of 4 km.

       ☐

   (b) Find the taxi fare for a return journey of 8 km with a waiting period of 1 hour.

       ☐

9. The table shows the postage rates for sending packages to USA by sea.

First 1 kg	$22
For every additional 100 g	$1.50

   Find the postage for sending a 2.5-kg package to US by sea.

       ☐

10. Roxanne types at a rate of 5 pages in 45 minutes.

    (a) How long will she take to type 1 page?

                                                      ☐

    (b) How many pages can she type in 1 minute?

                                                      ☐

    (c) Let y = the minutes and x = the number of pages. Write an equation relating the number of pages typed to the minutes.

                                                      ☐

    (d) Use the equation to find how long she will take to type 20 pages.

                                                      ☐

11. Sally took 8 minutes to type 416 words. Her rate of typing was ☐ words per minute.

12. Alan spends $300 every 2 months. At this rate, how much will he spend in half a year? ☐

13. Linda makes 48 candles in 8 hours. Alexia makes 13 candles in 2 hours. At this rate what will be their total number of candles from 4 hours of work? ☐

14. Raju and his friends rented a boat for $5 per hour. For how many hours did they rent the boat if they paid $35 altogether? ☐

15. Eva can type 50 words per minute. At this rate, how long will she take to type 1,800 words? ☐

16. Water flows out of a tank at the rate of 400 ml per minute. How long will it take for 7.2 L of water to flow out of the tank? ☐

17. The table shows the price of beef and chicken at a market.

Beef	$3.50 per lb
Chicken	$1.95 per lb

Mrs. Campbell bought $\frac{1}{2}$ lb of beef and 2 lb of chicken. How much did she spend?

18. The table shows rates of charges for renting a tennis court.

Monday to Friday	$3.50 per hour
Saturday to Sunday	$5.00 per hour

(a) David rented the tennis court for 3 hours on Wednesday. How much did he have to pay?

(b) Jim rented the tennis court on Tuesday and Saturday. He paid a total of $22. If he rented the tennis court for 2 hours on Tuesday, how many hours did he rent the tennis court for on Saturday?

BLANK

BLANK